# Fighting Fair Flash Cards

Glue or tape these cards onto 3" x 5" index cards for greater durability.

## 1. Focus on the problem.

State what is really bothering you.

## 2. Attack the problem, not the person

Use caring and respectful language

## 3. Listen with an open mind.

Do not interrupt. Do not use harsh language or a threatening tone of voice. Allow for disagreement.

# Fighting Fair Flash Cards

## 4. Treat the other person with respect.

Frequently restate the other person's point of view to show that you are listening.

## 5. Take responsibility for your reaction

Do not blame others, but focus on what you can do to solve the problem.

## 6. Do not commit "fouls"

(name-calling, blaming, any physical contact, threats, and so on)

# The Anger Thermometer

It is important to understand what makes you "hot" and what "cools" you down. Write in the people, places, and things that make you feel mad or calm.

**People, Places, Things**

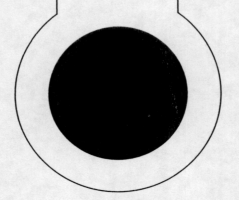

Boiling Over

Steaming Hot

Warm

98.6 (Normal)

Cool

Cold

Frigid

_____
_____

_____
_____

_____
_____

_____
_____

_____
_____

_____
_____

_____
_____

# The Therapist's Toolbox

## A Collection of Techniques for Counseling Children and Adolescents

by the editors of the *Child Therapy News*

Contributors:
Lawrence E. Shapiro, Ph.D.
David Greenwald, Ph.D.
Hennie M. Shore
Clary Wiesner, Ph.D.

**Childswork Childs**PLAY™

Secaucus, NJ

© 1998 Childswork/Childsplay, LLC, a subsidiary of
Genesis Direct, Inc.,
100 Plaza Dr., Secaucus, NJ 07094
1-800-962-1141

Printed in the United States of America

ISBN 1-882732-70-7

# Contents

# Preface

*Psychotherapy is one of the most confusing professions of our times. People generally agree on what therapy can and cannot do, but how it is done is a matter of much debate. For decades, the various schools of psychotherapy each felt that only it had the right theories and techniques, but in the last decade there has been more agreement on which methods work best with specific disorders and problems.*

*We are now on the threshold of a new era in psychotherapy, where it will become more of a science than an art. In the next decade, we will increasingly identify protocols of therapy that are the most efficient ways of helping clients, and within these protocols there will be specific techniques that will prove themselves to work better than others, depending on the age and development level of the client as well as the severity of the problem.*

*The Therapist's Toolbox is a step in that direction—an attempt to gather together the most frequently used and effective techniques in child and adolescent therapy, and to present them in a format that will make it easier for practitioners to select the best among them. In this first volume, we are presenting a cross-section of techniques, many of which are highly developed and empirically validated, and others of which are included because they are fun and innovative. In selecting the techniques, we tried to sample the spectrum of methodologies used with children and adolescents, from the traditional, behavior-oriented techniques to more humanistic approaches— and everything in between. To be included, each technique had to be unique and had to show effectiveness in working with specific disorders of children and adolescents. We hope that this book, and the books to come in the series, will help practitioners find and master the tools that they need to do their jobs with ease, certainty, and effectiveness.*

*The Editors*
*Child Therapy News*

# Active Listening

## When to Use The Technique

Virtually any type of problem will benefit from improved communication.

## Patient Age and Profile

This technique will work well with verbal children 9 years and older. Children who have verbal problems or attention disorders may have difficulty with this technique.

## How the Technique Works

Active listening is a way of reassuring the speaker that the listener is trying to understand what the speaker is saying and feeling. In "normal" listening, we often state our points of view as the speaker is speaking, in an effort to agree or disagree. Active listening requires that we put aside our reactions and give the speaker our full attention. Johnson and Johnson (1991) maintain that to listen to another person in this manner, you must face the person, stay quiet (until it is your turn to speak), think about what the person is saying, and show you understand.

The key to active listening is paraphrasing, or restating in your own words, what the other person feels and means. Paraphrasing helps you to avoid judging and evaluating, because when you are paraphrasing you are not passing judgment. Give the speaker lots of feedback that you understand the messages; communicate your desire to understand exactly what is being said.

Put yourself in the speaker's shoes and see the message from the speaker's perspective, and show your understanding and acceptance by nonverbal behaviors such as tone of voice, facial expressions, gestures, eye contact, and posture.

Be sure to use feeling words in your classifying statements. For example, you might say, "I think what you're saying is that you enjoy playing with

### Definition

Active listening is a technique used to improve communication between adults, children, or adults and children. To use the technique, the listener needs to suspend his or her own judgment and values while listening. The listener tries to interpret the content of the speaker's message, then "feed back" what he or she thinks the speaker is trying to say. This is done by paraphrasing the speaker's message. The listener does not offer an interpretation of what the speaker is saying, nor any opinion, advice, or questions. The speaker is then given the chance to verify whether or not the listener truly understood the message being conveyed.

Bobby, but you're frustrated because you think Bobby doesn't want to play with you, and you feel discouraged."

## Indicators/Measures of Success

The success with this technique is seen in the improved communication between the parties involved. The child will feel comfortable opening up further and exploring his or her feelings and thoughts in greater depth.

## Suggested Readings and Resources

Gordon, T. *Parent Effectiveness Training.* New York: Penguin, 1970.

Sorenson, D. *Conflict Resolution* and *Mediation for Peer Helpers.* Minneapolis: Educational Media Corp., 1992.

# Activity Group Therapy

## When to Use the Technique

AGT can be helpful with children and adolescents who are dealing with grief, have eating disorders, exhibit suicidal tendencies or juvenile delinquency, abuse substances, or have experienced parental divorce, sexual abuse, and so on.

## Patient Age and Profile

AGT is especially helpful for latency-aged children (ages 8 to 12) with behavior problems.

## How the Technique Works

It is assumed that as the children become more comfortable with the group, they will begin to see it as an idealized family and will gain insight into their own behavior by the discussions that follow the activities. The typical format of the group is a specific activity, which could range from videotaping a play to playing a game to woodworking. Since peer pressure is important to latency-age children, it is also assumed that this can have a corrective influence on the group members.

In conducting AGT, there are specific variables that can be manipulated in order to generate the interest and motivation of the group members, including:

- *The physical setting of the therapy room, including any toys, games, or equipment used for projects.* The permissive context of this technique calls for a setting in which children do not have to worry about being neat or damaging things. Equipment is usually kept in a locked closet and brought out by the therapist in order to provide some direction to the group when choosing an activity.

- *Group composition and balance.* The group should consist of children with a variety of behavioral and cognitive skills. Although the group members may all have behavioral problems, some should be at a higher developmental level so that they can guide the group as a whole toward more adaptive functioning.

- *Sex and age of the group members.* Groups usually consist of same-sex children who are approximately the same age. Since children who are

---

### Definition

Activity Group Therapy (AGT) is used as an approach for children who are aggressive or are acting out. Its basic premise is that latency-age children are most comfortable in groups. During group meetings, children participate in fun activities with the therapist and are given verbal praise. The group is generally "permissive," allowing the children a great deal of freedom in what is done and said.

significantly older than other group members (i.e., more than two years) will typically dominate the group, these members should be chosen with caution.

- *Sex of the therapist.* Traditionally the therapist is of the same sex as the group, but research has shown that opposite sex therapists can also be effective.

- *The actual group process used during sessions.* This can vary according to the needs of the group and the abilities of the therapist. Typically the group does activities for at least half of each session, sometimes as individuals and sometimes in pairs or sub-groups, with the rest of the session involving discussion about current issues and specifically about things that happened during the "activity" part of the session.

- Timing of group sessions. Groups are generally most effective when they meet at least twice a week for periods of six months or longer. The more frequently the group meets, the quicker it will coalesce into a surrogate family.

The basic mechanisms of AGT are:

(1) *Identification.* The dynamism of identification (copying or modeling behavior) is exerted through the therapist, group members, and the symbolic family formed by the group. To make identification possible, a warm, trusting, accepting, and confident relationship must exist between the therapist and the group. This permits competition with the therapist, and the power he or she holds over the group is often challenged, permitting the therapist to point out the inconsistencies of the children's words and actions. The children gradually become aware of their problems and also identify with other group members, since the group approximates the neighborhood "gang."

(2) *Reinforcement and presentation of alternate behaviors.* Based on the premise that the best way to increase a desirable behavior is to reinforce it, AGT promotes intrinsic, extrinsic, and social rewards. To modify behavior in AGT, the following steps are taken: (1) decide the target behavior, (2) determine how to measure the behavior and obtain a baseline, (3) select a desirable reward, (4) develop the plan with the child, (5) shape the desired behavior by rewarding successive approximations, (6) reinforce intermittently to consolidate gains, and (7) use fewer extrinsic reinforcers in the group play, thereby relying more on social reinforcers in the natural environment. After a behavior is modified within the group, behaviors at home and at school are examined and then modified.

■ *Insight.* To achieve insight, the child must have developed reasoning skills. This ability is facilitated in AGT through participation in conversations and discussion groups. The therapist's role in developing insight is to encourage discussion of real-life situations; to reality-test with the group; and to offer alternatives, along with the other group members, to behavior. In addition to insight resulting from verbal discussions, insight may develop from actions, feelings, and experiences; feedback provided by peers; and games used to help children learn lessons that are applicable to life.

## Indicators/Measures of Success

To measure the success of this form of therapy, Frank (1991) provides an example of a "typical" scene from a traditional activity group: "One need only imagine a rather typical scene in the traditional activity group when the children have their first argument in which both words and bodies are involved. The therapist, keeping an eye on both individuals and the group momentum, chooses to get up from his spot. As the affect mounts he atypically starts to sweep the floor near the argument. There is no discussion, no interpretation, and certainly no confrontation. In this way, the therapist provides a caretaking nonintrusive presence. Such therapist behavior can introduce useful identificatory figures to children who need such influences which have been absent in their lives.

"Children belonging to these groups are aware that the adult has 'intervened.' In addition, they are aware that they have been spared the anticipated reminder about good behavior or kindness to others they have come to expect from adults. They are now able to take advantage of what we would now call a 'new object experience.'"

## Suggested Readings and Resources

Frank, M. "Expanding Knowledge/Expanding Practice in Group Psychotherapy with Children." *Psychoanalytic Group Theory and Therapy: Essays in Honor of Saul Schiedlinger.* Monograph 7 of the American Group Psychotherapy Association Monograph Series. Madison, CT: International Universities Press, 1991.

Johnson, J., W. Rasbury, and L. Siegel. *Approaches to Child Treatment.* New York: Pergamon, 1986.

Reister, A., and I. Kraft, eds. *Child Group Psychotherapy, Future Tense.* Monograph 3 of the American Group Psychotherapy Association Monograph Series. Madison, CT: International Universities Press, 1986.

Schaefer, C., L. Johnson, and J. Wherry. *Group Therapies for Children and Youth.* San Francisco: Jossey-Bass, 1982.

Slavson, S. R., and M. Schiffer. *Group Psychotherapies for Children.* New York: International Universities Press, 1975.

# Assertive Discipline

## When to Use the Technique

This technique can be effective with many different behavioral problems.

## Patient Age and Profile

This technique works with children of all ages. It is important that the technique be tailored to the child's age. For example, sending a 5-year-old to his or her room for punishment will probably be effective, but the same punishment for a 13-year-old will probably not have the desired result.

## How the Technique Works

Assertive discipline is used when the usual manner in which a parent deals with a child is not working for a specific problem. The technique was developed by family/child counselor Lee Canter and his wife, Marlene Canter, a teacher. They initially developed the technique to teach new discipline skills to teachers and administrators. Realizing that parents needed the skills, too, they expanded the technique and developed a program for parents.

Canter outlines the steps of the technique in his 1985 book (see below). The first step in the technique is for the parent to take charge and assume the role of the "boss." The message the parent sends by assuming this role is that the parent loves the child too much to let the child misbehave. This role also involves giving the child positive feedback when he or she makes behavior changes. The three basic steps that make the technique successful include:

*Assertive communication.* Parents need to be taught to avoid ineffective responses. Ineffective responses include nonassertive responses ("Why won't you listen to me?") and hostile responses ("You're really going to get it this time!"). Instead, parents should use direct, firm statements, such as "Start your homework right now." The statement should be said in a very calm voice, and eye contact should be made (by gently turning the child's head, if necessary). Placing a hand on the child's shoulder is also a very effective way to communicate authority. Getting into an argument with the child always means that the child will win. Instead,

### Definition

Assertive discipline is a technique that teaches parents how to provide firm, consistent, and loving discipline for children. Parents are taught to effectively take on an authoritarian role with their children and consistently reinforce limits that have been set.

the parent should utilize the "broken record" technique and simply repeat the request calmly and firmly over and over in response to the child's attempt to argue. The final step in communicating assertively is to give the child positive attention when he or she is behaving well. This will reinforce the good behavior, and the child will not have to misbehave in order to get noticed.

***Backing up words with action.*** Parents need to decide what consequences they can and will enforce when their child does not comply with an assertive request. This should be something that the child will not like (but will not be physically or psychologically harmful). The most important part of this step is to provide the consequence each time it is indicated. Most parents will provide it at first and see immediate improvement. However, when the behavior reoccurs (usually at a lower rate than it originally occurred), parents typically do not want to punish the child because they are so pleased by the improvement over the baseline. It is critical that the child consistently receive the consequence each time he or she misbehaves. If the parent threatens the consequence and does not follow through, the consequence will simply be another empty threat. A child will also "test" his or her parents to see if they really mean it or if they can be persuaded to lift the consequence.

***Laying down the law.*** To effectively do this, parents need to have a written system for how they are going to handle really problematic situations. The plan should list the behaviors the parents would like to see changed and what the consequences will be. Having such a plan prepares the parent and builds his or her confidence. The plan should have a list of different consequences that are ranked in order of severity. Misbehaviors can also be ranked in order of severity, and a corresponding consequence can then be utilized.

Another effective system to use in laying down the law with children is to draw up a contract. The contract stipulates what reward the child will receive for behaving according to certain guidelines. The contract can be written down and signed by the child (if old enough) and parent and then posted where the child can keep track of how close the child is to getting the reward.

To implement the system of laying down the law, the parents should set up a conference with the child. This should be done when the parents are calm and no other siblings are present. The parents should state what behavior they would like to see changed and what consequences will occur if the changes are not seen. A list of the changes (and consequences) can be posted in the child's room to serve as a reminder for the child. The contract system (to reward positive behavior) can be implemented at the same time, and this contract can be posted as well. When problems arise, the parent needs to assertively communicate with the child and implement consequences that have been decided upon before-hand. When the child is not misbehaving, he or she should be praised and given positive support.

## Indicators/Measures of Success

This technique is generally successful when the parent learns to effectively and consistently reinforce consequences. It may take differing amounts of time for different children to respond to the technique. A child who responds "I don't care" when consequences are implemented may take longer to respond than a child who cries and carries on. However, with consistency, both types of children will respond to the technique, and an improvement in behavior will be seen.

## Suggested Readings and Resources

Canter, L. *Assertive Discipline for Parents.* New York: Harper & Row, 1985.

# Assigning Family Tasks

Technique

In-session tasks are designed to have the family reach a solution while in the office, with minimal coaching from the therapist. The goal is to have a successful communication experience. Tasks given as homework are used to help the family develop and repeatedly use behavior patterns outside of the sessions.

## When to Use the Technique

Almost any kind of problem can lend itself to a family task assignment that has been well thought out. Minuchin and others found that task assignment worked especially well for helping lower socioeconomic class and highly disorganized families. These families had organizational deficits; therefore, basic task performance was found to be more helpful than symbolic psychological techniques appropriate for more well-to-do families. For these families, identifying and mobilizing the most constructive forces in the family can be enhanced by assigning tasks that may change habitual coalitions or destructive behavior patterns.

## Patient Age and Profile

Family members of all ages can benefit from this technique.

## How the Technique Works

In structural family therapy, from which this technique comes, symptoms are viewed as resulting from dysfunctional family structures (i.e., an overinvolved mother/underinvolved father, too much distance between parents, an alliance between a parent and one particular child, etc.). Assigning tasks becomes a focused way to change the family structure. If there is one underinvolved parent, that parent is assigned a task that will bring that parent into more contact; if the parents have too much distance, they may be assigned to spend an evening at the movies together, etc. In-session tasks may give the therapist greater control over monitoring the carrying out of the task, but homework is often seen as more useful because it takes the goals of the therapy home with the family and allows change to continue after the session.

### Definition

Family therapy is based on the entire family making behavioral changes. Many therapists assign tasks for the family members to perform during or between sessions. Tasks that might be assigned during the session would be for the family to plan an outing together; tasks for between sessions might include the parents going out on a date, assigning one parent as the homework mentor, or even making appointments with social agencies in the family's neighborhood.

## Indicators/Measures of Success

One of the advantages of this technique is that there is a clear measure of its success—either the task was completed or it wasn't. If a family or client is consistently noncompliant with these assignments, the therapist needs to consider the secondary gains of the symptoms for the family or what other problems may be standing in the way of task completion.

## Suggested Readings and Resources

Madanes, C. *Strategic Family Therapy.* San Francisco: Jossey-Bass, 1981.

Minuchin, S., et al. *Families of the Slums: An Exploration of Their Structure and Treatment.* New York: Basic Books, 1967.

Minuchin, S., and H. Fishman. *Family Therapy Techniques.* Cambridge, MA: Harvard University Press, 1981.

# Behavioral Contracting

## When to Use the Technique

Behavioral contracting is usually used for relatively mild behavioral concerns, including following instructions, hygiene, chores, doing tasks without being asked, losing weight, doing homework, and being more responsible.

## Patient Age and Profile

Written contracts are successful with children over age 5, who are at least partially motivated to improve their behavior. They usually do not work with oppositional or defiant children or those with other conduct disorders, unless they are used in combination with more intensive therapeutic strategies.

## How the Technique Works

Contracting works best when it is used with a limited number of specific behaviors or tasks. Contracts should not be used for a task that the child is already successfully completing, but rather in areas where the child is having difficulty and has so far experienced limited or no success. Contracting is one of the simplest forms of behavior modification, as it motivates children with a sense of responsibility and structure.

The contract uses a number of important psychological principles, such as (1) rewarding positive behaviors and ignoring negative ones (behavioral therapy); (2) spending time and energy to help the child understand how much the adult values good behavior (client-centered therapy); and (3) documenting success (behavioral therapy).

## Indicators/Measures of Success

The technique is considered successful when the contract is followed and the behavior is measurably improved.

## Forms

Behavioral Contract for Young Children, page 189.

Behavioral Contract for Older Children, page 190.

### Definition

Behavioral contracting, also called contingency contracting, is a technique used to help solve a variety of problem behaviors. Creating a behavior contract involves choosing a specific task that needs to be worked on and a reward that will be supplied for successfully completing the task. Both are written down, and the terms of the contract are negotiated. After the terms of the contract have been met for the specified amount of time, the reward is given.

## Suggested Readings and Resources

Dardig, J., and W. Heward. *Sign Here: A Contracting Book for Children and Their Parents.* Bridgewater,
NJ: F. Fournies & Associates, Inc., 1976.

# Bibliotherapy

## When to Use the Technique

Use this technique whenever you have access to appropriate materials. There are books that deal with virtually every mental health concern of children.

## Patient Age and Profile

This technique can be used with any child old enough to read. The books selected should be tailored to the child's developmental level as well as reading ability. Children who have severe difficulty reading due to a learning disability, mental retardation, or autism may be too frustrated by their struggle to read to gain any benefit from the material.

## How the Technique Works

Bibliotherapy can be practiced in a variety of ways. Books can generally be classified into four groups: therapeutic metaphors, books that model appropriate behaviors and solutions, interactive books, and books that provide specific information. Children can be given specific books on a topic, or offered a variety of books. Children can either read the books alone, or they can be read aloud with the therapist, a parent, or in a group or classroom situation. Bibliotherapy is based on learning theory as well as insight-oriented therapies. It is a nonintrusive technique that is highly effective with motivated clients.

Books have been recommended for patients since the 1800s, when Benjamin Rush recommended novels be used to help mentally ill patients. In 1916, Samuel McCord Crothers coined the phrase "bibliotherapy" in an article for *Atlantic Monthly,* and a paper by William Menninger, which was read before the American Psychological Association in 1937, discussed the technique.

## Indicators/Measures of Success

Bibliotherapy is an educational technique, and as such should provide the child with new information and attitudes that contribute to new behaviors. These behaviors can be measured by appropriate scales or observational techniques. More informally, this technique might be

| Definition |
| --- |
| Bibliotherapy is a technique that uses books as a therapeutic supplement to therapy. In the technique, the therapist may either suggest specific books or offer an array of books to children. The books chosen generally deal with the topic that the child is struggling with and offer the child the chance to gain more information and a different perspective on their problem. |

considered successful when children reread the assigned books and willingly discuss what they have learned from their reading.

## Suggested Readings and Resources

Bernstein, J. *Books to Help With Separation and Loss*. New York: R. R. Bowker Company, 1983.

# Brainstorming

## When to Use the Technique

The solution(s) to most problems encountered by school-age children can be found by using this technique.

## Patient Age and Profile

School-age children and adolescents can benefit from this problem-solving technique.

## How the Technique Works

Brainstorming is effective only as part of a problem-solving process. The group puts forth ideas without discussing or criticizing them. The atmosphere should be nonjudgmental, no matter how outrageous the ideas seem, in order to elicit different kinds of thoughts that may ultimately lead to the best solution. The likelihood of finding a solution increases with the number of suggestions produced.

Children should feel free to offer ideas that are not necessarily reflections of what they think and feel. Ideas should be recorded and displayed where they can be seen by the group. When ideas have been recorded, the list should be reviewed and like ideas grouped together. Items should be simplified, if appropriate, and items that seem most relevant should be discussed in detail.

In addition to being used to find solutions to problems, brainstorming can be used to define problems, to find out what problems children want to work on, to find causes of conflict, and so on. Children should keep in mind that even when a plan or solution is chosen, it may prove to be "not quite right" further down the line. Modifications may need to be made in the future.

The basic rules for brainstorming include:

1. *Say anything that comes to mind.* A crazy idea may seem nonsensical, but it may provide the seed for the solution that is finally adopted. "Beyond their occasional usefulness," writes Robert Bolton in People Skills, "zany ideas often serve as relaxants to a group, and may thereby foster greater creativity."

### Definition

Often, when confronted with a problem, it is difficult to see alternative solutions, options, and possibilities. Brainstorming is a method of generating alternative solutions to a problem. It helps develop a child's ability to produce many responses to a question, and it demonstrates that children working together on a problem can generate a greater variety of solutions than one child working alone. The key is to direct the flow of creative thinking energy toward finding several possible solutions quickly, usually in no more than five minutes.

2. *Don't judge your ideas or the ideas of others, even when they seem like great solutions.* Evaluation thwarts creativity. It makes people defensive and more likely to keep their ideas to themselves.

3. *Don't limit your ideas by trying to have them make sense.* Don't clarify or seek clarification. Explanatory remarks interfere with the rapid and creative generation of possible solutions. When people try to explain what they mean, the idea flow begins to slow down.

4. *Expand on each other's ideas.* Without asking the person to clarify, think of a "piggyback" idea. Brainstorming generates a lot of incomplete ideas. Some of the best solutions have come from adding to or combining ideas.

5. *See how many creative ideas and solutions you can come up with, and don't restrict your thoughts in any way.* The person recording the ideas should not be an editor or a censor—he or she should record the idea in the speaker's words.

6. *Avoid attaching names to ideas.* Put everyone's ideas on the same list (children's and teacher's). "All parties contribute to the climate which nurtures creativity, each puts forth ideas which triggers the thinking of others—so, in fact, even if one person makes a contribution which is adopted, it is a group effort," Bolton maintains. "Focusing on who gave words to the idea is dysfunctional."

## Indicators/Measures of Success

When brainstorming is used, children will be able to generate a number of alternatives to a given problem. When children have learned this skill and it can be applied to their problems, the technique can be considered successful.

## Suggested Readings and Resources

Bolton, R. *People Skills: How to Assert Yourself, Listen to Others, and Resolve Conflicts.* New York: Simon and Schuster, 1979.

Drew, N. *Learning the Skills of Peacemaking.* Rolling Hills Estates, CA: Jalmar Press, 1987.

Korb, K., S. Azok, and E. Leutenberg. *Self-Esteem and Life Skills Plus.* Beachwood, OH: Wellness Reproductions Inc., 1992.

Prutzman, P., et al. *The Friendly Classroom for a Small Planet.* Philadelphia: New Society Publishers, 1988.

# Circular Questioning

## When to Use the Technique

As the name implies, the Milan Group started in Italy and as such is uniquely suited to certain cultural types of families. In general, families that are overly involved with each other respond better to this approach than families that have become symptomatic because of too little engagement. Circular questioning begins the process of teaching a family to think in a "we are all responsible for each other" circular manner rather than the more limited good guy-bad guy presentations of individual pathology.

## Patient Age and Profile

Very young children will find it hard to participate in this procedure. School-age children, however, will be able to join in with their own perceptions of others in the family. Adolescents will greatly appreciate being called upon to offer their considerable expertise on their parents and the other members of the family. The Milan Group has had its most noteworthy successes with anorectic patients and first break psychotics and schizophrenics.

## How the Technique Works

The Milan Group views part of its therapeutic agenda as helping families differentiate between the two levels of meaning and action. Therapeutically, it believes that introducing new information will lead to new actions and new patterns of behavior that will reflect the new beliefs.

Families in circular questioning investigations will allow the therapist to ask the same question of several people and thus probe more deeply into differences as well as interconnectedness while being nonconfrontational and nonthreatening. This type of questioning often produces change in the family in and of itself while providing information to the therapist.

The other aspects of the Milan Group's approach include hypothesizing (a formulation by the therapist or therapy team as to what is responsible for maintaining the family's problems), neutrality (the therapist's need to stay allied with all family members and not overemphasize a connection with one member or one part of the family), positive connotation (seeing

### Definition

This technique focuses the family's attention on relationships and connections rather than individual symptomology. It is a family therapy interview procedure developed by the Milan Group. In circular questioning every question is asked as it relates to differences in family perceptions, to address differences in perception about important events or relationships. The approach is called circular because usually a third person is being asked about the relationship between two other people. (Example: How would your mother and father differ in response to your sister's temper tantrums? Rate each family member on a 10-point scale as to how angry he or she would get.)

all behavior, and especially symptomatic behavior, as contributing to the family equilibrium), and rituals (tasks that make formerly covert patterns overt or change them).

## Indicators/Measures of Success

Hopefully family members will be able to discuss and discover previously unrecognized ways in which they influence each other. Individual differences will also be elicited; this will allow each member to grow more fully in his or her own way. Families will become better observers of family interactions. Circular questioning can continue, with new data constantly generating new questions that are probed in the same manner. As such, this is more a style of investigating, a way of asking questions that frames the agenda and the family's view of what is happening and what needs to happen to bring about change.

## Suggested Readings and Resources

Andolfi, M. *Family Therapy: An Interactional Approach.* Plenum: New York, 1979.

Boscolo, L., et al. *Milan Systemic Family Therapy: Conversations in Theory and Practice.* New York: Basic Books, 1987.

Selvini-Palazzoli, M. *Self-Starvation.* New York: Jason Aronson, 1978.

# Client-Centered Play Therapy

## When to Use the Technique

Client-centered play therapy is especially effective with children who have problems expressing their feelings concerning specific traumatic experiences, such as loss of a loved one, child or sexual abuse, or their parents' divorce.

## Patient Age and Profile

Client-centered play therapy usually takes place with children from the ages of 4 to 12. Nondirective play therapy is an "open-ended" technique, and as such is not typically used for problems that can be addressed more directly. It is most commonly used with such chronic problems as childhood depression, trauma and post-traumatic stress syndrome, elective mutism, and anxiety and separation issues.

## How the Technique Works

In client-centered play therapy, the therapist provides toys for the child and permission to play with them. Boundaries are set concerning which areas are off-limits and which ones are accessible. The child knows that the therapist is available for talking or playing if the child so desires. The therapist presents himself or herself as warm, friendly, and accepting, and refrains from judging the child or invalidating the child's thoughts, feelings, or fantasies. The therapist sits at the same height as the child (usually on the floor) and follows the child's direction in participating or not in play.

The basic assumption of client-centered play therapy is that people are inherently good, and each person is driven toward self-actualization. Virginia Axline believed that a negative environment subverts this drive, resulting in maladaptive behavior. To remedy this, Axline provides a positive, optimal environment in which the child can begin to grow once again. Exposure to this nurturing and supportive environment allows the child to once again start the self-actualization process. Once this process is started in the play therapy sessions, the child can begin to apply this increased level of functioning to situations in everyday life.

Axline stated that the therapist must be able to provide a warm, genuine, and empathic milieu in order for client-centered play therapy to be

### Definition

Client-centered play therapy is synonymous with nondirective play therapy and is based on the principles of nondirective therapy popularized by Carl Rogers, Virginia Axline, and others. The goal of this type of play therapy is to allow the child to bring feelings to the surface, where he or she can face them and learn to control them. Allowing the child to express feelings in this way results in growth and psychological maturity. As the child matures, the realization of "selfhood" occurs.

effective. The therapist needs to allow a degree of permissiveness in order to allow the child to be natural, yet clear boundaries must be set concerning appropriate and inappropriate behavior. Axline believed that it was important that the child be aware of his or her responsibility in the relationship.

In setting up a playroom for the child, the following guidelines should be observed:

- Choose toys that can be played with in a variety of ways. Leave room for the child to create his or her own toy—for example, provide building toys rather than a prebuilt castle.

- Include toys that allow the expression of feelings that are usually forbidden in everyday life, such as aggression. Punching bags, rubber knives, and guns may all serve this purpose.

- Provide toys that can be played with alone or in combination. Avoid those that require the participation of two people. This allows the child the choice of either including the therapist or not.

- Decide which toys you are comfortable with and which ones are too messy, noisy, etc. Fingerpaints may allow the child to freely express himself or herself in new ways, but they may also leave an unacceptable mess in the room.

- Older children should be given age-appropriate toys, such as target games, board games, or miniature bowling or basketball games. Outdoors games may be especially appropriate for children of this age.

In the first session, the therapist educates the child about play therapy. The child is told that this is his or her special room for an hour a week—a place where he or she can say or do almost anything. This allows the child freedom while setting the stage for limit-setting that may prove necessary later. The child is shown where the toys are and given permission to play with them. The therapist also lets the child know that the therapist is available for play or talk at the discretion of the child. Some children who are very shy or hesitant may need to see the therapist engaging in an activity with the toys before they are comfortable initiating play of their own.

In the next few sessions, the child will explore the limits and possibilities of play therapy. Aggressive behavior may emerge during this stage, or passive and dependent behaviors may be played out. Children who have been severely abused by adults may need the therapist to initiate open-ended games with them. The therapist should remain attentive to the child, even if the child chooses not to interact with the therapist. If the child remains silent—for example, coloring alone in a book—the therapist should comment on the process of the child (i.e., "You're carefully coloring her shoes to match her dress").

In the middle sessions, regressive behaviors tend to occur. The child may want to play at being a baby or pretend to feed a doll. It appears that this is the stage where children build trust in the therapist and begin to relax in sessions.

In later sessions, children tend to be more reality-oriented. Fantasy play gives way as the child begins to act out more realistic scenarios. Aggression is at a low level during this stage, and when it appears, it tends to be related to specific incidents. More social behaviors begin to emerge, and children who previously cheated or were poor losers are more likely to be honest and better sports about losing.

Specific behaviors on the part of the therapist are critical for success in this technique:

(1) *Empathic responding.* It is important that the therapist respond to body language and verbal expression by the child. An empathic response notes the child's behavior or reaction and validates the child's experience.

(2) *Structuring.* Enough information must be given to the child in order to let him or her know what is appropriate in the therapy session and what is not. In the first session, the child should be told how long the sessions will last, how often they will occur, which areas are off limits, etc.

(3) *Setting limits.* Very clear and well-defined limits should be set around inappropriate behaviors. If a child is stabbing the therapist with a sharp toy, rather than stating, "You are not allowed to hurt me," the therapist should more specifically state, "I won't let you stab me with the soldier's sword." If the child continues the behavior, the therapist should reiterate the rule ("Remember, I told you that you are not allowed to stab me with the soldier's sword") and let the child know what the consequences will be if the behavior continues. Consequences might include taking away the toy or giving the child a time-out. If the behavior occurs again, the threatened consequence needs to be carried through with a verbal explanation of why this action is being taken. ("Remember I told you that I would take the soldier away if you stabbed me with his sword again.")

Client-centered play therapy attempts to restore balance in the child's life, allowing him or her to resume healthy growth. The play therapist seeks to facilitate the child's self-exploration and self-growth by participating in the child's play in a warm, friendly, and empathic way. Certain limits are placed on the child's behavior, and within these limits the child is encouraged to be self-directive. Rather than initiate action, the play therapist waits and responds when the child initiates play with the therapist.

## Indicators/Measures of Success

The success of client-centered play therapy can be determined by using instruments that measure the presence of specific symptoms, such as the Children's Depression Inventory.

## Suggested Readings and Resources

Axline, V. *Play Therapy.* Boston: Houghton Mifflin, 1947.

O'Connor, K. *The Play Therapy Primer.* New York: John Wiley & Sons, 1991.

Schaefer, C., and K. O'Connor, eds. *Handbook of Play Therapy.* New York: John Wiley & Sons, 1983.

# Cognitive-Behavioral Play Therapy

Technique

## When to Use the Technique

CBPT has been successfully used with children who have toileting issues (particularly encopresis and enuresis), speech and language problems (especially elective mutism), post-divorce issues, fears and phobias, and sexual abuse issues.

## Patient Age and Profile

CBPT is generally used with children from the ages of 3 through 10. Children at the upper end of this age bracket may be reluctant to engage with the therapist in play unless age-appropriate games are suggested.

## How the Technique Works

CBPT is based on the theory that children can learn to change their own behavior and become active participants in their own treatment. The term was coined by Susan Knell, Ph.D., who advocates this technique as a time-limited approach to treating disorders of young children. It is brief, structured, directive, and problem-oriented. It is also a multimodal approach, blending techniques of the three major schools of children's therapy.

Issues of control, mastery, and responsibility are introduced by the therapist for the child's examination. Through learning to identify and modify potentially maladaptive beliefs, children can experience a sense of personal understanding and empowerment. The therapist uses modeling, role-playing, and behavioral contingencies as interventions. The CBPT therapist also serves as an educator, teaching new skills to the child, and provides praise and interpretation in the belief that doing so will help the child to acquire greater understanding and new skills and behaviors.

The following are some of the principles outlined by Knell (1993):

- CBPT involves the child in treatment via play. The therapist seeks to actively engage the child in the therapy process, addressing any issues of resistance or noncompliance as they arise. Engaging the child allows the therapist to communicate directly with the child instead of through parents or other adults in the child's life.

**Definition**

Cognitive-behavior play therapy (CBPT) is a play therapy technique that combines cognitive-behavioral interventions and traditional play therapy techniques.

- CBPT focuses on the child's thoughts, feelings, fantasies, and environment. This allows the therapist to focus on situation-specific factors (such as phobias or bedwetting) as well as the child's feelings about the problem. Feelings and thoughts are both considered along with situational and environmental issues.

- CBPT provides a strategy or strategies for developing more adaptive thoughts and behaviors. It gives the therapist a way to teach the child new coping skills. Children can begin to replace their old, maladaptive ways of coping with more adaptive approaches. Using toys and puppets, a modeling technique is employed to teach positive self-statements to the child. The puppets can also present scenarios similar to those faced by the child and then model appropriate and adaptive responses.

- CBPT is structured, directive, and goal-oriented, rather than open-ended. The therapist first establishes what goals the child and family would like to accomplish through CBPT. The therapy then focuses on meeting these goals as defined by the family.

- CBPT incorporates empirically demonstrated techniques. It draws from the techniques used in cognitive and behavioral therapies. One of the most documented techniques, modeling, is the basis of much of CBPT. Modeling allows the therapist to demonstrate things in a concrete, nonverbal, yet specific way. This is especially helpful in working with preschoolers.

- CBPT allows for an empirical examination of treatment. CBPT provides a way for the specific effects of each intervention to be measured and assessed. This allows the treatment to be tailored very effectively to each individual client.

The behavioral interventions used in CBPT include:

*Modeling.* Modeling is a technique that exposes the child to some-thing or someone (person or puppet/stuffed animal) who demonstrates the behavior to be learned. This is an especially important technique when working with very young children who do not understand more verbally oriented treatments. Modeling has been shown to be an effective way for children to acquire, strengthen, or weaken behaviors.

*Role-playing.* The use of role-playing allows the child to practice skills and behaviors with the therapist and receive feedback. This technique is usually more successful with school-age children than it is with preschoolers. For these younger children, role-playing and modeling techniques can be combined. For example, if a child is shy, the therapist might have two puppets role-play a scene in which one of the puppets is also shy, yet begins to try to interact.

*Positive reinforcement.* This usually involves rewarding the child for using a desired new skill or behavior. Behavior that is positively reinforced tends to increase, and this principle is capitalized upon in CBPT.

*Shaping.* If a child is attempting to learn a new skill or behavior, he or she may struggle with the learning process involved in developing the new skill. The therapist will praise approximations of the new skill, commenting in a positive way on each attempt at mastering it.

*Stimulus fading.* This is used when the child is able to act in the desired way but does so only in certain settings or with certain people. The therapist helps the child to transfer his or her positive and adaptive skills in one setting to another setting.

*Extinction.* Extinction is not a technique that teaches new behaviors; rather, it is used in conjunction with a reinforcement program. To use extinction, the therapist withholds reinforcement in an attempt to extinguish a certain behavior.

*Differential reinforcement of other behavior (DRO).* To use this technique, the therapist reinforces behavior that is inconsistent or incompatible with the undesirable behavior. If the child is not punished for the undesirable behavior but is instead rewarded for the replacement behavior, the reinforced behavior is likely to increase.

*Cognitive change strategies.* This technique is used to help children change their faulty cognitions. The child is helped with hypothesis testing in which he or she experimentally tests out thoughts, beliefs, and assumptions. Preschoolers do best with this technique if concrete examples are used and fewer open-ended questions are asked. Through play the child can experiment, looking at evidence, exploring alternatives, and examining consequences. Children can also be taught positive self-statements during play, using self-affirmations such as "I am doing a good job." This cognitive approach also helps children to develop the language to express their thoughts and feelings.

The play therapy used in CBPT is directive and is used as a context in which to apply appropriate cognitive and behavioral interventions.

## Indicators/Measures of Success

Creating a behavioral baseline and measuring symptom remission is an important part of CBPT.

## Suggested Readings and Resources

Berg, B. "Cognitive Play Therapy for Children of Divorce." *Innovations in Clinical Practice,* Vol. 8, P. Keller and S. Heyman, eds. Sarasota, FL: Professional Resource Exchange, 1989.

Knell, S. *Cognitive-Behavioral Play Therapy.* Northvale, NJ: Jason Aronson, Inc., 1993.

_____. "To Show and Not Tell: Cognitive Behavioral Play Therapy." *Play Therapy in Action.*
T. Kottman and C. Schaefer, eds. Northvale, NJ: Jason Aronson, Inc., 1993.

Russo, S. "Adaptations in Behavioral Therapy with Children." *Behavior Research and Therapy,* 2, 43-47, 1964.

# Cognitive Mediating Techniques

## When to Use the Technique

Angry children and children who are overly aggressive in their initial reactions to negative stimuli can benefit from these techniques.

## Patient Age and Profile

These techniques are most effective for preschool through early elementary school-age children with anger-control problems.

## How the Technique Works

Cognitive mediating was designed to teach children to use an internal dialog by following the way they normally develop internalized speech. First, they talk out loud while doing a specific task. Then they whisper to themselves, mouthing the words as they do the task. Finally they think to themselves as they do the same task.

Although children can clearly learn to think before they act in the research lab or the therapist's office, it is less common for this new cognitive/behavioral skill to transfer and generalize to the child's natural environment. In other words, children may use self-guiding speech in activities or controlled role-playing in the therapist's office, but they may continue to act impulsively in their classroom, playground, or home, unless learning this technique includes practice in the child's actual environment.

There are many techniques that have been shown to be successful in helping children apply cognitive mediating in their day-to-day lives. They all include practice, or using the technique in the place(s) where the problem is occurring. Two examples include:

- *The Stop, Think, and Proceed Technique.* Described by Dr. Kenneth Dodge of Vanderbilt University as a technique to deal with impulsivity in the classroom, this program uses the concrete imagery of a traffic light to deal immediately with the impulsive behavior of children.

  When a child misbehaves, he or she is directed to stand in a red circle ("red light") and count to 100, taking deep breaths in order to relax.

### Definition

Cognitive mediating techniques are representative of a type of cognitive intervention that has been particularly popular with impulsive children. It is assumed that these children do not "think before they act" and therefore do not use an internal dialog to "mediate" between their desires and their behaviors, as do other children of the same age.

Next the child proceeds to a yellow circle ("yellow light"), where he or she is told to think about the behavior and what to do next. Finally, the child stands in a green circle ("green light"), where he or she tries out a solution to see if it works. For example, if the child hit someone, he or she would have to apologize. If the child took something that belonged to someone else, he or she would have to make reparation.

An individual child using this program could instead use a picture of a traffic light with red, yellow, and green circles and simply hold a finger on each circle while completing the exercise.

■ *The Turtle Technique.* This technique was originally designed for use in the classroom to help young children control their anger. When children are angry or upset they are told to think of a turtle withdrawing into its shell, pulling its arms and legs tightly to its body, closing its eyes, and lowering its head. In this position, the child cannot be aggressive, and older children can also be taught to think about other solutions to the immediate problem.

The child is taught a four-step process in learning the turtle response as a substitute for aggression: (1) identify specific situations or cues that normally result in an aggressive response; (2) practice using the Turtle Technique in role-play situations; (3) practice responding to a "turtle" sign by the teacher or other adult (such as a hand that is closed in an upside-down fist); and (4) the child should be expected to cue himself or herself and use the technique in appropriate circumstances, being rewarded when reporting its appropriate use.

### Indicators/Measures of Success

These techniques are effective because they use an effective yet flexible psychological principle; they are concrete and can be used anywhere; they allow children to deal with their emotions in a physical as well as a cognitive way; and they are fun. In addition, they work on the metaphoric as well as the concrete level. For example, in the Stop, Think, and Proceed Technique, the three colors of the stop light represent stages, and as the child moves from one to another, he or she progresses toward a higher stage of functioning while learning to control his or her behavior. Further, these techniques can help parents and teachers to respond effectively and thoughtfully instead of through harsh discipline measures, which often contribute to aggression.

### Forms

Stop Light Card, page 211.

## Suggested Readings and Resources

Camp, B. *The Think Aloud Program.* Champaign, IL: Research Press, 1981.

Slap-Shelton, L., ed. *Child Therapy Today.* King of Prussia, PA: The Center for Applied Psychology, Inc., 1994.

Technique

# Cognitive Restructuring

## When to Use the Technique

Cognitive restructuring is especially useful with depressed children and adolescents.

## Patient Age and Profile

Children aged 10 and older can learn to recognize and change their automatic self-defeating thoughts.

## How the Technique Works

Two theories of psychotherapy—the rational emotive therapy (RET) developed by Albert Ellis, and the cognitive treatment originated by Aaron Beck—suggest that older children (10 and up), adolescents, and adults can learn to change their feelings and behaviors by learning new ways to talk to themselves. These two theories use different language to describe the same phenomena—a patient can learn to identify dysfunctional or irrational thoughts and replace them with more realistic thoughts and ones that lead to more adaptive functioning.

The underlying principle behind cognitive restructuring is that thoughts are learned much the way behaviors are learned. The "ABC" theory of personality directs the therapist's approach and the client's understanding of how the treatment will help. Ellis explains that there is an original activating event (A), which is then associated with a belief (B), which triggers a specific emotional response (C).

According to RET theory, the activating environmental event does not directly cause the child's emotional reaction and behavior, but rather it is the child's beliefs about the event that cause the emotional and behavioral consequences. Therefore, disputing (D) the child's belief system through reasoning and other objective techniques will result in a new way of thinking and behaving.

Beck and his colleagues note that when patients associate an irrational or dysfunctional belief with a particular event, this becomes an automatic thought, and each time the event occurs, the associated thought occurs with it. When these automatic thoughts are distorted, however, they lead to dysfunctional feelings and behaviors.

---

### Definition

Cognitive restructuring is a technique that focuses on the power of changing one's thoughts to change feelings and behaviors. Unlike cognitive mediation, this technique assumes that children have an internal dialog (i.e., they talk to themselves) that guides their behavior, but the thoughts that they have are often irrational or dysfunctional.

---

Take, for example, the child who sees his or her parents making a fuss over the new baby in the house. The child has the automatic thought, "They like the baby better than me," every time he or she sees the parents with the baby. Without intervention, the event and the belief become a self-fulfilling prophecy. Every time the child sees the parents with the new baby, he or she finds another way to justify the irrational belief: "See, I was right. Look how happy they are. They are much happier with the baby than with me." As the child becomes angrier and angrier and begins to act defiantly toward the parents, the prophecy becomes true—the parents have more and more difficulty enjoying the company of their son or daughter.

Beck argues that these automatic thoughts are dysfunctional because they are based on a variety of cognitive distortions, such as:

*overgeneralization* ("Everyone hates me.")

*absolute thinking* ("I'll never learn how to do long division.")

*focusing on negative details* ("My hair looks ugly. People will make fun of me."

*disqualifying positive occurrences* ("Sharon invited me to her party, but that's because her mother made her invite everyone in the class.")

*minimizing or maximizing the importance of occurrences* ("I gave a dumb answer in class today; now everyone will think I'm stupid.")

*overpersonalizing the reaction of others* ("Dad never finds time to be with me. He must think I'm a big disappointment.")

There are many techniques that can help children (and their parents) confront their automatic, irrational, and dysfunctional thoughts. Cognitive restructuring is an educational technique, which involves explaining the theory outlined above to the child and teaching him or her to identify and change automatic thoughts or beliefs as a way to change inappropriate affect and behavior.

After children understand the basic concepts on which this technique is based, they are helped to see the original events that caused their dysfunctional thoughts and beliefs as well as how their beliefs now distort their perceptions of new experiences.

One technique advocated by Beck and his colleagues to help patients identify this process is called the triple column technique (see the triple column technique form). In this technique, the therapist guides the patient toward identifying his or her automatic thoughts and writing them in the first column, exploring why these are distorted in the second column, and deciding on rational (non-distorted) responses in the third column.

## Indicators/Measures of Success

When the identification and changing of automatic behaviors and thoughts become "rote," and the child's behavior is more appropriate, this technique can be considered successful.

## Forms

Triple Column Technique, page 215.

## Suggested Readings and Resources

Beck, A. *The Cognitive Therapy of Depression.* New York: Guilford Press, 1979.

Ellis, A. "Rational-emotive Therapy." *Current Psychotherapies* (3rd ed.). Itasca, IL: Peacock, 1984.

Technique

# The Compromise Game

## For example:

*Player 1:* Two people are fighting over an apple.
*Player 2:* Split the apple in half and give each person a half.

*Player 2:* Two brothers are in a boat, and one wants to row all the time.
*Player 3:* Each brother takes one oar.

*Player 3:* A family of three is riding in a car on a long trip. Two people think that it is too hot, but the third person says it is too cold.
*Player 1:* Each person could get half an hour when they can control the temperature. Make sure that the person who is too cold has a blanket and that the people who are too hot are sitting near a window.

## When to Use the Technique

Children who need help with social skills and conflict resolution can be helped by this game.

## Patient Age and Profile

This game is designed for children over age 7 to play together (two or three players are ideal).

## How the Technique Works

Conflict-resolution skills are being taught today in schools around the country. One important skill that is taught in such programs is the ability to create "win-win" compromises, where two adversaries both end up getting something each wants. The compromise game was devised to teach children how to create "win-win" compromises in the face of a conflict and as a vehicle for them to practice this skill in a nonthreatening setting so that when a conflict arises, compromise will come about naturally.

## Indicators/Measures of Success

When children learn to compromise as an alternative to conflict, the goal of this game will have been achieved.

---

### Definition

Before you begin to play this game, talk to the children about the importance of creating compromises. Give them some examples, and ask them if they can contribute some examples of their own.

How to play: Player 1 states a problem or conflict using a word that begins with the first letter of the alphabet. The word should be the name of an object. The player to the left must then come up with a compromise whereby each person in the conflict gets something that he or she wants.

## Suggested Readings and Resources

Sorenson, D. *Conflict Resolution and Mediation for Peer Helpers.* Minneapolis: Educational Media Corp., 1992.

# Cooperative Learning

## When to Use the Technique

Children who are having problems with conflict resolution can benefit from this technique.

## Patient Age and Profile

Elementary school students can benefit from this novel approach to learning.

## How the Technique Works

Johnson and Johnson (1991) identify five basic elements that are essential to cooperative learning. These elements are what differentiates cooperative learning from traditional discussion group formats. The authors base their explanation of these elements on the example of a set of math problems students are given to solve. Students are placed in groups of three. The instructional task is to solve each story problem correctly and understand the appropriate strategy for doing so. With this understood, the five elements of cooperative learning are ready to be put in place.

1. *Positive interdependence.* Students must believe that they are linked with others in a way that one cannot succeed unless the other members of the group succeed; that is, they "sink or swim" together. Within the lesson, the teacher creates positive goal interdependence by requiring group members to agree on the answer and strategies for solving each problem. Positive role interdependence is structured by assigning each student a role:

- The reader reads the problems aloud to the group.

- The checker makes sure that all members can explain how to solve the problems.

- The encourager encourages all members to participate in the discussion and share their feelings and ideas.

Resource interdependence is achieved when the group is given one copy of the problems to be solved, and all students work on the problems individually while sharing their insights with each other. Positive reward

| Definition |
| --- |

Many teachers think that cooperative learning is simply putting students in groups and having them talk while they do their assignments, having the students who finish first help the slower ones, or assigning a project to a group where one student does all the work, but everyone takes the credit. The essence of cooperative learning is much more than being physically near other students, discussing material with others, helping others, or sharing materials with others, although each of these is important in the process. When composing cooperative learning groups, it is desirable to make them heterogeneous with regard to academic ability, ethnic background, or physical disability.

interdependence is structured by giving each group 5 points if all members score above 90 percent on the test given at the end of the unit. Goal interdependence is achieved through the mutually shared group goal.

2. *Face-to-face promotive interaction.* This exists when students help, encourage, and support each other's efforts to learn. They do this by:

- orally explaining to each other how to solve problems;
- discussing the nature of the concepts and strategies they are learning;
- teaching what they know to each other;
- explaining to each other the connections between what they are learning now and what they have learned in the past.

The teacher also provides encouragement for the students to exchange ideas and help each other learn.

3. *Individual accountability.* This exists when the performance of each individual is assessed and the results are given back to the group and the individual. It is important that group members know who needs more assistance in completing the assignment and that they cannot "hitchhike" on the work of others.

Effective ways of structuring individual accountability include giving a test to each student and randomly selecting one student's work to represent the efforts of the group.

4. *Social skills.* These are essential for groups to function effectively and include leadership, decision-making, trust-building, communication, and conflict-management skills. Johnson and Johnson maintain that these skills should be taught as purposefully and precisely as academic skills, as cooperative learning is new to many students, and they may lack the social skills for it. To practice these skills, the roles as defined in Step 1 are rotated. When the teacher sees students engaging in social skills, he or she records it or verbally praises the student.

5. *Processing.* This is also essential so that students can analyze how well their learning groups are functioning and what can be done to improve the process. At the end of the period they ask:

- What is something each member did that was helpful for the group?
- What is something each member could do tomorrow that would be even better for the group?

Such processing enables members to focus on group dynamics, facilitates the learning of social skills, ensures that members receive feedback on their participation, and reminds students to practice the small group skills required to work as a cooperative group.

## Indicators/Measures of Success

In stressing the benefits of cooperative learning, Kreidler (1984) writes that Jean Piaget "tells us that interaction is the most important aspect of learning, and research shows that children in cooperative learning situations do academically as well as or better than students in competitive or individualized programs."

## Suggested Readings and Resources

Johnson, D., and R. Johnson. *Teaching Students to Be Peace-makers*. Edina, MN: Interaction Book Co., 1991.

Kreidler, W. *Creative Conflict Resolution*. Glenview, IL: Scott, Foresman and Co., 1984.

Technique

# The Cooperative Robot Game

The Cooperative Robot Game is a fun game for three people to play, and it can be learned in a few minutes. The youngest player starts in the middle and holds hands with the other two players. Now all three players must function as one. The player in the middle is the "brain," and the players on the sides must coordinate their hands to do what the brain wants. Try these activities:

1. Make a peanut butter and jelly sandwich and feed it to all three "heads."

2. Using a mirror, draw a picture of what you look like joined together and cut out the picture.

3. Do a simple chore such as sweeping the kitchen floor or making a bed.

## When to Use the Technique

Cooperative games are helpful for all children, but they are particularly recommended for children who are noncompliant or who have difficulty in controlling their temper.

## Patient Age and Profile

Children at any age can benefit from playing cooperative games. However, this type of activity is most likely to generalize to other behavioral situations when children are young.

## How the Technique Works

Cooperative games work on a classic behavioral principle: When children practice a behavior in a natural environment and are reinforced for this behavior, they will begin to exhibit it more often.

## Indicators/Measures of Success

The usefulness of cooperative games in teaching cooperative behaviors has been primarily studied through observational techniques. When used as part of a treatment plan, an increase in cooperativeness would be measured by a standardized behavioral checklist.

## Suggested Readings and Resources

Orlick, T. *The Second Cooperative Games Book.* New York: Pantheon Books, 1982.

---

### Definition

Cooperative games are defined as games during which "everyone wins or everyone loses." This type of game helps children develop a sense of belonging in a group or team, and avoids the confrontations and conflicts that often come with competitive games. Several studies have shown that when classes of children are taught cooperative games on the playground, there is less aggression during play time and improved behavior in the classroom.

# Dance/Movement Therapy

With children, DMT is most commonly used as a way to facilitate communication and to understand and integrate feelings. For example, it can be used to help depressed or traumatized clients find a safe way to express their feelings of frustration, hurt, and anger. For aggressive or antisocial children, it can provide a means for them to express gentler, more prosocial feelings and interact with others in a more appropriate way. A second goal of DMT with children is to encourage appropriate interactions by reflecting, mirroring, and labeling the child's behavior. With developmentally disabled children, DMT can be used as a way to facilitate nonverbal communication and may be used to aid verbal communication as well.

Marian Chace is generally regarded as the founder of DMT, although many other people were influential in the field. Chace organized the American Dance Therapy Association, becoming its first president in 1966. Most of the DMT techniques developed by Chace are still in use today. Other early dance movement therapists who contributed to the field are Francizka Boas, Mary Whitehouse, Trudi Schoop, and Alma Hawkins.

## When to Use the Technique

Dance movement therapy can be used as an adjunctive therapy with many children who have developmental, behavioral, or emotional disturbances, including autistic and mentally and physically handicapped children. It tends to be used in very severe cases, where more traditional "talking" therapies have failed or when the child shows a particular inclination toward the expressive arts.

## Patient Age and Profile

DMT can be used with children of any age.

## How the Technique Works

Stanton-Jones (1992) describes the five essential theoretical principles of DMT:

(1) The body and mind are in constant reciprocal interaction, and therefore change on the movement level affects overall functioning.

---

### Definition

Dance/movement therapy (DMT) is an art therapy in the same vein as music, art, and drama therapy. The American Dance Therapy Association defines dance/movement therapy as "the psycho-therapeutic use of movement as a process which furthers the physical and psychic integration of an individual." There are four major schools within the DMT field: psychodynamic, Jungian, ego-psychoanalytic, and Gestalt. DMT is used as an adjunct to other forms of therapy and is especially useful with clients who have a hard time responding to strictly verbal forms of therapy.

Dance movement therapists thus are continually encouraging clients to connect verbal insight with movement experience by encouraging free association and interpreting the movement.

(2) Dance movement therapists believe that movement reflects personality. Research suggests that movement can highlight psychopathology or other aspects of the personality. Movement is thought to be deeply related to both self-knowledge and self-transformation. In order to capitalize on the nonverbal dimension of personality development, the therapist will mirror a client's movement. This technique is believed to recapitulate the childhood developmental process of learning who we are by seeing how others experience us.

(3) The relationship of the dance movement therapist to the client is believed to be central to the effectiveness of the technique. This relationship both enables and supports change on the part of the client. The dance movement therapist responds to the client by mirroring, synchronizing, amplifying, and interacting with the client's movements. This creates a powerful bond between the therapist and client.

(4) Movement, like dreams, drawings, slips of the tongue, and free association, can be evidence of material from the unconscious. This material includes ideas, thoughts, and feelings that have been repressed and thus are out of immediate awareness. Interpreting the movement and the material it signifies can lead to therapeutic change.

(5) The last principle is that the act of improvising movement is inherently therapeutic in that it allows the person to experience new ways of moving. This leads to a new and different sense of being in the world and allows the person to experience his or her own creativity. The unconscious provides a source of creative inspiration, and feelings from the unconscious can be brought out and integrated with the personality.

## Indicators/Measures of Success

Since DMT with children is done as an adjunct to other forms of therapy, it is difficult to assess how successful the DMT has been in and of itself. Generally success is measured anecdotally and qualitatively, and the technique is often seen as important in developing a positive relationship with the therapist.

## Suggested Readings and Resources

Stanton-Jones, K. *An Introduction to Dance Movement Therapy in Psychiatry.* London: Tavistock/Routledge, 1992.

# Developmental Play Therapy

## When to Use the Technique

Developmental play theorists believe that this technique is helpful for a wide variety of problems, but it is probably best used with children whose symptoms can be traced to inadequate or negligent parenting, as well as for children with severe problems in interpersonal relationships.

## Patient Age and Profile

Developmental play therapy has been used with preschool-age children as well as with adolescents. It is sometimes used with very hard to reach children, such as those with those with pervasive developmental disorders. Because this type of therapy involves physical contact of various forms, it should be used under strict supervision and with explicit parental consent.

## How the Technique Works

The technique is loosely based in psychodynamic theory, which promotes the concept of "regression in service of the ego." This concept suggests that taking clients to early stages of development can help them reconstruct new ego strengths, which will then benefit them in developing interpersonal relationships.

Developmental play therapy was described by three different theorists. In 1962, Des Lauriers set the groundwork, which was refined by Jernberg in 1979. Around the same time as Jernberg, Brody coined the phrase "Developmental Play Therapy." Although there are some differences in their practices, these theorists believed that nurturance that was not provided in early life could be provided in later life and could be used to address a variety of emotional disorders.

## Indicators/Measures of Success

Developmental play therapy combines setting limits and giving structure to the child's play, while at the same time providing nurturance in the form of physical comfort and deep emotional caring.

### Definition

Developmental play therapy seeks to provide the caretaking interaction that was inadequate in the child's early life. To achieve this, the therapist assumes a caretaking role toward the child during the course of the play therapy.

## Suggested Readings and Resources

Brody, V. "Developmental Play: A Relationship Focused Program for Children." *Journal of Child Welfare*, 57(9), 591-599, 1978.

Des Lauriers, A. *The Experience of Reality in Childhood Schizophrenia*. New York: International Universities Press, 1962.

Jernberg, A. *Theraplay*. San Francisco: Jossey-Bass, 1973.

O'Connor, K. *The Play Therapy Primer*. New York: John Wiley & Sons, 1991.

# Differential Attention

## When to Use the Technique

This technique is especially helpful with ADHD children.

## Patient Age and Profile

Differential attention is used with preschool or early elementary school-age children who are displaying disruptive behavior problems such as noncompliance, defiance, and physical aggression.

## How the Technique Works

A frequent question asked by parents of ADHD children is: "When should I ignore an inappropriate behavior, and when should I punish it?" The principle of differential attention addresses this concern.

One of the great paradoxes in behavior management is that lecturing, scolding, and other negative reinforcement techniques often increase the incidence of negative behavior rather than decrease it. Adult attention (whether good or bad) is one of the most powerful reinforcers that a child can receive. Even negative consequences that follow misbehavior can actually serve as positive reinforcers for the misbehavior, as the child receives attention from the adult.

Furthermore, many children who exhibit "bad" behavior do not receive enough attention for being good. Indeed, parents of ADHD children often neglect to pay heed when the child is "good" as they are so tired of attending to the child when he or she misbehaves. The parent who reacts frequently to the bad and pays little attention to the good is inadvertently teaching the child that negative behavior is a good way of receiving attention.

Parents must first determine which misbehaviors can be safely ignored and which misbehaviors should be directly addressed with discipline. Unfortunately, this is not an easy task. A child may be grimacing, banging on walls, jumping up and down, screaming, etc., all for the purpose of obtaining the parent's attention. The parent needs to be able to bear the behavior and ignore it every time it happens.

### Definition

Differential attention is the application of adult attention following an occurrence of a desired behavior and the removal of an adult's attention after an undesired behavior. It involves giving positive attention to all good behavior, removing attention from (ignoring) all negative behavior that is harmless, and providing negative consequences for behaviors that are very disruptive or potentially harmful. When used, differential attention selectively attends to good behavior and more serious misbehavior and ignores trivial misbehaviors.

The following examples show how difficult behaviors might be treated:

| Ignore | Discipline |
|---|---|
| Beth Ann begins to yell and scream. | Joyce kicks her brother. |
| Larry is making paper airplanes and throwing them around the house. | Derrek refuses to sit at the dining table. |
| Minh makes strange faces and oinks at the dining table. | Bobby throws glass bottles at his sister. |
| Keith throws sofa cushions around the house. | Billy rips the curtains off the windows. |

After parents determine which misbehaviors they will ignore and which they will discipline, it is important that they be consistent. A parent who ignores a certain behavior should ignore it every time, not ignore it sometimes and react with discipline at other times. In order for differential attention to work, the parent must be ready to positively reinforce (with attention) good behavior as often as possible. Simply ignoring selected poor behavior will not give the child incentive to behave; incentive to behave exists only if the child knows that the return from behaving exceeds that from misbehaving.

## Indicators/Measures of Success

The success of the use of differential attention can be determined by an increase in the child's appropriate behaviors as he or she learns which behaviors need to be decreased in frequency or eliminated. A side benefit is that differential attention helps both parent and child become aware of specific behaviors and their effects. It also helps the parent to slow down, begin to enjoy the child more, and to relate to the child on his or her level. Conversely, as the parent reacts positively to the good behaviors, the child begins to enjoy interactions with the parent, and the parent's value as a source of reinforcement increases. In essence, time spent with each other becomes "quality time."

## Suggested Readings and Resources

Forehand, R., and R. McMahon. *Helping the Noncompliant Child: A Clinician's Guide to Parent Training.* New York: Guilford, 1981.

Hembree-Kigin, T., and C. B. McNeil. *Parent-Child Interaction Therapy.* New York: Plenum, 1995.

# The "Do Something Different" Task

## When to Use the Technique

This task works most effectively with seeming "lost causes," or where the complaint is "I've tried my best." It is often used with oppositional children because it does not provide an easy target to oppose.

## Patient Age and Profile

This should not be the first intervention tried but should seem to come when all else fails. It can be suggested to either children of all ages or teachers but is most effective with parents who have sometimes become engaged in power struggles where they are attempting to do "the right thing" over and over, to no avail. Thus parents can be told to back off when confrontation has failed and reward when punishment has failed.

## How the Technique Works

This technique, like many clever interventions, has its roots in communications and systems work. It is similar to pattern interruption, another procedure that works on directly changing behavior that has become habitual and nonproductive.

Doing something different can mean almost anything that changes the usual and predictable. Children are often more spontaneous than adults, and so adding a measure of unpredictability to adult response can be a useful reaction. For example: A mother who fought with her son every morning before school about getting to the bus stop on time was instructed to do something different. In this case, she decided to stand outside and wait for the bus herself, something the boy found embarrassing. In a short while he started to get to the bus stop early, without the lengthy harangues and arguments that had preceded this "difference."

## Indicators/Measures of Success

When problems can be looked at and approached differently, creative new solutions may be found. If the no-win aspect of an impasse can be overcome, then the technique has been successful. If the usual fight or reaction can be changed once, then there has been a success experience that can be built upon.

---

### Definition

An axiom of brief therapy is that "if it works, keep doing it." This task is based on the opposite: "If it is not working, do something different." In this case, the actual difference is less important than "that it is different."

When dysfunctional behaviors occur, they become problematic through repetition. When clients feel hopeless or at an impasse, it is important to validate their experience and then suggest that they try something new. It almost doesn't matter what it is, as long as it is something new or different. By doing something different, the habitual negative behavior becomes interrupted and changed.

The "do something different" task can be offered as an experiment, to be tried for a little while but not necessarily forever.

As in many brief therapy techniques, success is sought in very discrete, small behaviors. Change is not attempted in large, global, personality dimensions but rather on specific troubling, repetitive habits. In this view if there is a small change, that change will become self-reinforcing and will lead to larger changes.

## Suggested Readings and Resources

de Shazer, S. *Putting Difference to Work.* New York: W. W. Norton, 1988.

_____. *Keys to Solutions in Brief Therapy.* New York: W. W. Norton, 1985.

Haley, J. *Uncommon Therapy: The Psychiatric Techniques of Milton Erickson, M.D.* New York: W. W. Norton, 1973.

# The Domino Effect Game

## When to Use the Technique

This game can be helpful with children who have conduct disorders, ODD, or antisocial behaviors.

## Patient Age and Profile

Children 10 and older should be able to understand the metaphor of the game.

## How the Technique Works

Cabe explains that the realization of behavioral cause and effect is the first step in establishing an internal locus of control, a concept of social learning theory. The experience of playing this type of game in a therapeutic context can potentially make an emotional "imprint" that can lead to insight and a change in behavior.

## Indicators/Measures of Success

The success of this type of technique can really only be measured by an objective behavioral rating scale filled out by teachers and parents. Often this type of therapy can result in the child or teenager feeling that he or she has changed, but the adults around the child do not perceive the change. For this reason, self-report inventories are not reliable.

## Suggested Readings and Resources

Cabe, N. "Consequences: Reaching the Oppositional Defiant Adolescent." H. Kaduson & C. Schaefer, eds. *101 Favorite Play Therapy Techniques.* New York: Jason Aronson, 1977.

### Definition

Many children have difficulty understanding the cause and effect relationship between behaviors and the consequences of those behaviors. Neil Cabe (1977) discusses how a game of Domino can be used as an experiential metaphor to show how one behavior affects another, and how moving just one domino can break the link in the chain. Each domino is identified as representing a particular behavior in a chain of events. For example, domino 1 might represent talking back to a teacher; domino 2 might represent the teacher making a sarcastic comment back; domino 3 might represent refusing to do work during that period; and so on.

Technique

# The Draw-a-Dream Technique

## Definition

In this procedure, the therapist shows the child a cartoon drawing of a child asleep, with a speech or thought balloon over his or her head. The therapist tells the patient that the child in the cartoon (who is given the same name as the patient) is having a bad dream, and then asks the child to draw the dream. The therapist links the distressing feelings of the dream to the life events with which the child is coping, paying particular attention to parental conflict.

The second step of this procedure consists of asking permission to show the drawing of the dream to the parents. In this way, parental understanding of the connection between family problems and the child's distress may be "drawn" in a nonconfrontational way.

## When to Use the Technique

Many families present children's problems as seemingly independent of other family conflicts. The therapist is asked to "fix the child" but leave the family alone. This task is often at odds with the therapist's goal of helping to effect change in the family context, thereby helping the child in a more long-lasting way. With such families, it is difficult for the therapist to elicit information the family might well regard as irrelevant. In families with open hostility and quarreling, or families that receive secondary gains by maintaining symptoms in the child, this technique can circumvent the family's usual defensive stance.

## Patient Age and Profile

The child needs to be of sufficient age to be able to draw in a rudimentary way or at least to describe what he or she might draw in the cartoon character's dream. It is also important for the therapist to have a general sense of the family issues that may be affecting the child's behavior or of its contributions to the child's problems. In families with anger, conflict, or strong emotional forces under the surface, this technique can help the child represent, understand, and, with the therapist's skill, present the child's fears and upsets to the family in a way that can be heard.

## How the Technique Works

Stress on children can be considerable in hostile families or those in which there is a great deal of parental conflict. In these families, as systems therapists have long noted, a symptomatic child acts as a conflict avoider for the parents, who may join together to focus on the child and ignore their own conflict. In this way symptoms are maintained. Children are often unaware of the effects of their environment on their own feelings and behavior.

This approach attempts to introduce the nature of family interactions, first to the child and then to the parents. If the child draws a dream of a big monster destroying the house, the therapist can ask if that is how things feel at home sometimes. Questions can then be raised: "Does your father's anger feel like the monster's sometimes?" The child may then elaborate on how bad the fights at home can be sometimes. With permission to show the parents the picture so that they can understand what is worrying the child, the parents are helped to see how their conflicts affect the child, and new understandings and behaviors can be achieved. The draw-a-dream technique thus allows the therapist to avoid the parent-child problem perspective and offer the child a means of expressing a graphic and concrete representation of his or her world that is difficult for parents to ignore.

## Indicators/Measures of Success

There are two levels on which this technique may succeed. First, the child may get relief from understanding and gaining insight into the source of the upsetting feelings, helping the child to comprehend the meaning of otherwise unfathomable behavior. Success at the family level is attained when the parents get a glimpse into the inner world of their child. Their awareness of family problems and their effect on their child can help cause them to seek alternatives to previously nonproductive attempts to get help.

## Suggested Readings and Resources

Tonge, B. "Draw a Dream: An Intervention Promoting Change in Families in Conflict." *The International Book of Family Therapy.* New York: Brunner/Mazel, 1982.

Technique

# Enactment

## Example

A mother begins a session by expressing concern and fear over how her husband recently lost his temper and physically threatened their son. The father says that the boy was not doing an assigned task, and the escalating conflict ultimately led him to pushing the son up against a wall and choking him. The therapist asks for a reenactment of the event, and the father and son recreate their fight.

The first advantage of this technique is that the therapist is able to see what really transpired, which lends far more immediate, emotional validity to an otherwise verbal recounting. The therapist can then intervene: What was the father thinking? What, if anything, from his own life did this remind him of, and what would he want to do differently? The therapist can further ask the mother and son to hold the confrontation pose so that the father may view this tableau from the other side of the room, to recognize more clearly the emotional and historical relevance it has for him.

## When to Use the Technique

Structural family therapy, which gave rise to enactment as a technique, primarily works with families that are less verbal, more active, and more chaotic than those families that are highly socialized, educated, and affluent.

This approach requires a great deal of activity on the part of the therapist, but it also allows the therapist to get to the "heart" of the family rather than just listen to the family's words regarding their problems. It can change the dynamics of families that are struggling with delinquency, anorexia, school truancy, violence, and other serious problems. Enactment allows the problem into the session, so that the family structure may be worked on through the interactions of the family members.

## Patient Age and Profile

For structural change to occur, it is usually necessary for the entire family to be present for the enactment, including children and adults.

Grandmothers, aunts, or cousins are often included in inner city families where these participants may have an important structural role.

## How the Technique Works

Structural family therapy regards symptoms as reflections of faulty family structures. In effect, the problem is less important than how people deal with it—who talks to whom and in what manner, where the coalitions are, what the usual structural ways of dealing with the problem have been, etc. This approach focuses on how the structure of the family may interfere with the solution of a problem.

The first parts of the enactment are called "spontaneous transactions." These are the naturally occurring interactions between family members: mother nagging son and son consequently withdrawing; children fighting until a parent intervenes; parents disagreeing about discipline. For the second step the therapist applies pressure while the interactions are occurring, to see where changes might be made. The therapist might tell a mother to "make the children play quietly" without the father taking over in his usual way. During this step the family might become even more out of control or dysfunctional due to the therapist's prodding. This leads to the third step, which is an alternative transaction, during which the therapist keeps up the pressure to try something different from what the family has been doing. The therapist does not take over the parental functions; rather, he or she continues to pressure the parents to do their job more effectively.

## Indicators/Measures of Success

The first measure is an experiential one: Was the family able to get into the enactment? If it is a spontaneous repeat of a typical behavior pattern from home, then the answer is clear; if the therapist has asked the family members to re-enact a scene that already happened, then he or she needs to be attentive to the accuracy of the recreation (asking all participants for feedback on the action), the emotional responses of the actors, and especially who in this scene might be replaying old scenes from their own childhood.

The second measure of success is whether any structural change was able to be noted from this enactment. Was the family able to see the repetitive nature of family patterns, and was it able to learn alternative ways of handling difficult situations?

## Suggested Readings and Resources

Minuchin, S., and H. Fishman. *Family Therapy Techniques.* Cambridge, MA: Harvard University Press, 1981.

Nichols, M. *Family Therapy: Concepts and Methods.* New York: Gardner Press, 1984.

Real, T. *I Don't Want to Talk About It: Overcoming the Legacy of Male Depression.* New York: Scribner, 1997.

# Family Council

## When to Use the Technique

Family councils can help family situations where communication is disorderly and where each member feels unheard, misunderstood, or unacknowledged. Families that exhibit frequent power struggles may benefit from learning this procedure. Those that find it hard to stay on track during a discussion are also good candidates for this approach.

## Patient Age and Profile

This is an approach that can have benefits for a whole range of families with children of all ages. It is important for the therapist to stress that family councils are for the benefit of all and that concerns addressed in these council meetings be relevant to all members.

## How the Technique Works

Families become caught up in contests around a particular conflict, which then tends to block all other useful communication. The problem can take over the life of a family. The family council is based on the premise that democratic methods in family life will encourage respect among all family members, increase cooperation (because all will have a say in decision making), increase involvement with each other (because they are all involved in a meaningful activity), and help develop a sense of "us" while respecting differences and individual personalities.

As a regular family ritual, councils can go a long way toward helping families change their communication style from blaming to problem-solving and from ignoring to coming to terms with issues.

The rules and requirements of the council are:

1. The meeting must be held at a regular time and place without interruptions and distractions.

2. Everyone is invited, but no one is forced to attend. However, absentees must abide by the decisions of those who do attend.

3. Decisions made at meetings are final unless overturned in future meetings.

4. Everyone can propose agenda items. Sign-up sheets for these may help.

### Definition

This method was designed to foster discussion at family meetings. These meetings are formal, with specific rules that are meant to improve communication and help solve problems in general. Family meetings allow free communication between family members; they avoid emotional showdowns and violence in the family, teach parents and children democratic means of resolving conflicts and settling problems, and encourage the maintenance of an orderly and peaceful home. Family councils are prescribed by the therapist as a homework task.

5. The agenda is limited to anything that concerns the children, family activities, or the family unit as a whole (i.e., not business or investment issues). Parental issues may include chores, curfews, visiting friends, etc. Children may want to discuss having more independence, greater flexibility in doing chores, and television rules.

6. Chairmanship is rotated.

7. Sibling issues may be brought up, including hurt feelings, etc.

8. Consensus is sought rather than majority wins.

9. All must participate in carrying out decisions.

10. Meetings must focus on problems; verbal attacks on each other are forbidden.

### Indicators/Measures of Success

Success should result in everyone feeling more listened to, at a minimum. Greater respect for other's positions, better communication, and improved problem-solving skills are all also measures of success.

### Suggested Readings and Resources

Dreikurs, R., S. Gould, and R. Corsini. *Family Council.* Chicago: Henry Regnery, 1974.

Manaster, G., and R. Corsini. *Individual Psychology.* Itaska, IL: Peacock, 1982.

# Family Photos

## When to Use the Technique

This technique is most helpful for dealing with two situations. First, if the therapist has had a difficult time being let in by the family, this can speed up his or her joining in the emotional life of the group. Secondly, if a family can see only the negative things with each other or with a particular member, this gentle reminder can help them remember better times. This can also be an effective introduction to family therapy by getting the family used to seeing connections between members and between past and present events.

## Patient Age and Profile

This technique can be used with any verbal members of a family. Baby pictures, older generation pictures, special events, and daily activities can all give information to the therapist and family. Virtually all families have photos, and they are universally enjoyed for their nostalgic value. If certain family members are noted by their absence from the shots, questions will arise as to that person's importance to the family—or whether they are the only competent photographers in the bunch!

## How the Technique Works

The basic rationale for this procedure is the notion that the therapist can learn from it more of the family's history. Meanwhile the family members, in looking at their shared past together, will be better able to comprehend what is happening and can learn to deal with each other more productively.

The therapist has a wealth of possible information here, from both the content of the photos as well as the process of how they are presented. In what order were the pictures shown? What is the emotional tone during the viewing: embarrassed, joyful, anxious, sad, interested, etc.? How much does the family enjoy this trip down memory lane? Crucial family dynamics, including alignments, coalitions, communication, roles, and structure can be revealed by a discussion of just one picture.

### Definition

In this technique the family is asked to bring in a specified number of photographs that are meaningful to each member. There is then a go-around, with each person describing the photos which he or she selected. The therapist may elicit the "who, what, where, when, and how" of each photograph. Questions that may then be asked include the impact of the family's past on the present problem, who was included in the selections, and noteworthy times in the family's history. Information on family structure, styles, and communication patterns can all be gleaned using this nonthreatening approach.

## Indicators/Measures of Success

The success of this technique lies in the changing of a previously held negative assumption, for example, "My father never liked me." With photos of a younger son and father engaged joyfully in activities or a father taking obvious delight in his infant's reactions as evidence, a child or adolescent may rethink his or her relationship with that father.

Another indicator of success is that by sharing their memories with the therapist and each other, family members consequently trust the therapist more and feel greater warmth toward each other. Basically this is a no-lose procedure for the therapist; at worst he or she will have a great deal more information about this family with the technique than without it.

## Suggested Readings and Resources

Akert, R. *Photoanalysis*. New York: Wyden, 1974.

Anderson, C., and E. Malloy. "Family Photographs: In Treatment and Training." *Family Process,* 15 (2), 259-64, 1976.

Ferber, A., et al. *The Book of Family Therapy*. Boston: Houghton Mifflin, 1973.

# Family Puppet Interviews

## When to Use the Technique

A variety of children's problems, such as anxiety, bedwetting, fighting, and school phobias, can be explored less threateningly when the members can "hide" behind the puppets.

## Patient Age and Profile

This is a technique most suitable for very young children, as older children will feel that it's too "babyish," and parents will usually feel too inhibited to do this with them. Even in the presence of young children, parents may resist because they will most likely recognize the activity as symbolic of their own family situation.

## How the Technique Works

The idea here is similar to storytelling or family drawings—to involve the family in an activity where they are brought together to have fun and to give the therapist and each other information on how they feel and how they view their relationships.

An interesting variant of the technique can be the therapist setting up a scene to demonstrate what he or she assumes to be the basic patterns or underlying feelings in a family's interactions. In this nonthreatening way the therapist might show the family how they are being overly combative or overly controlling.

## Indicators/Measures of Success

The successful use of the technique should result in the family being less defensive, more involved in each other's lives, and more creative in finding new solutions to old problems.

## Suggested Readings and Resources

Irwin, E., and E. Malloy. "Family Puppet Interviews." *Family Process*, 14, 179-91, 1975.

Ariel, S. *Strategic Family Play Therapy.* Chichester, England: Wiley, 1992.

### Definition

As the name implies, puppets are used in this technique. The therapist asks one member of the family to make up a story using puppets. The puppets are chosen by the therapist for their symbolic representation of the family members. The therapist can thus get clues as to conflicts and emotional issues the family is experiencing.

Technique

# Family Sculpture

This technique is a fun, active way of engaging the family for diagnostic purposes. For example, it may be used to dramatically represent issues that the family is working on. Both the final result of the sculpture (content) and the way the "sculptor" uses the others (process) are explored in the therapy. It is worth noting who the sculptor arranges as domineering or meek, touching or clinging. A lively debate may follow this exercise.

An alternative is for the therapist to arrange the family the way he or she sees its members and then elicit feedback from the family as to the accuracy or usefulness of his or her perceptions. In either case, this technique is designed to provide information to all on mutual perceptions and possibly help the family see rigid or persistent patterns that limit their growth and flexibility.

Another approach might be to have the family members arrange each other the way they wish or would like the family to be in relationship to each other.

## When to Use the Technique

This technique is especially useful for nonverbal families or families where words are used to block rather than enhance communication. Adolescents make particularly adept sculptors because of their growing awareness of family truths and their enjoyment in manipulating their parents. Younger children are usually unaware of family patterns, and parents are often nervous about losing their dignity in such an active manner. However, once the ice has been broken by a family member, usually everyone wants his or her own turn.

## Patient Age and Profile

Family sculpture can be used with any imaginable type of family—single parent, extended, step—and with almost any kind of problem to show the structure of the group. Preferably three or four members should be present, although furniture can be used to signify missing members. If a family member feels strongly about not "sculpting" or even participating, his or her wishes must be respected. Whenever presenting this

---

**Definition**

In family sculpture the therapist asks the members of the family to arrange each other to show their relationships. Either one family member's viewpoint is elicited, or each is asked, in turn, to move the other people around until a living sculpture is formed, to show how each person in the family sees the others at this particular point in his or her life. The therapist may glean much useful information from observing how close people are, who is in alliance with whom, what (if anything) they are doing (i.e., scolding, cowering, hugging, threatening, entangled, etc.), and how involved they seem to be in doing this task.

approach, the therapist should adopt an inviting, playful, exploratory attitude to increase the likelihood of participation.

## How the Technique Works

The tableau that is created by each family sculptor represents that person's symbolic view of family relationships. How each person sees the family is important to understanding that person's place in the family and how he or she experiences the others. Many non-verbal people who have a great deal of difficulty with the question: "How do you see this family?" or "Where do you fit in?" can show the therapist and other family members their answers through this technique. Although this perception is seldom enough to begin to bring about change, the therapist can actively use the information gathered to help bring about greater closeness or distance, inclusion or disengagement, with varying family members.

An underlying assumption of this technique is that family patterns of relationship are often linked with symptomatic behavior. If this is true, the fundamental patterns in the family may need alteration in order to change the behavior. A further assumption of this method is that creativity, expressiveness, and communication are useful qualities for the understanding and solution of family problems.

## Indicators/Measures of Success

Like many family techniques, this one is designed to be a no-lose proposition. If the family or one of its members cooperates, there is bound to be new information (how this person sees the family); if the person does not cooperate, there is also information about that person's acceptance of the therapist, participation in treatment, or even their commitment to the family. Since this technique is primarily designed to provide information in a fun way, it is hard to "fail." Obviously, it is most successful if the family members do engage with each other, even laugh about being moved around, and make remarks such as, "I never knew that's how you saw things. I'm going to try to change things for the better because of this new view."

## Suggested Readings and Resources

Satir, V. *Peoplemaking*. Science and Behavior Books, 1972.

Simon, R. "Sculpting the Family." *Family Process,* 11:49, 58, 1972.

Technique

# Fighting Fair

## When to Use the Technique

Children with social skills deficits as well as those who need help with conflict resolution can benefit from this technique.

## Patient Age and Profile

Elementary age and middle-school age children can be taught to use this technique.

## How the Technique Works

Fighting fair in the family or at school does not refer to physical fighting but to verbal fighting, which can be just as harmful. In addition, anger expressed through fighting does not necessarily indicate a serious psychological problem. Fighting has always been one way that people resolve conflict, even though most people find it unacceptable. From a psychological viewpoint, we must accept the fact that children (and adults) will fight at times, but we must teach them to "fight fairly."

The underlying concept of fighting fair assumes that when children are angry, they do not communicate clearly. Fighting fair provides a framework for resolving conflict and frustration in a way that builds rather than tears down relationships. It allows anger to be expressed in a safe, healthy, conflict-reducing manner.

Fighting fair can be taught at home and in school. Children can use it any time they are involved in a fight. Following are some of the more important rules in fighting fair.

Do not commit "fouls." Fouls are weapons that put people on the defensive and cause conflict to escalate, including hitting, pushing, biting (anything physical); blaming ("Don't blame me—Sara did it," "It's all your fault"); name-calling ("You never do anything right, stupid."), threats; not listening; revenge; excuse-making; and not taking responsibility.

When the child is really angry, give him or her time to cool down. Children should be encouraged to find acceptable ways to cool down, such as taking a walk, playing with a pet, screaming into a pillow, or calling a friend.

| Definition |
| --- |
| Learning to fight fair is a form of cognitive behavior modification that teaches children to attack the problem and not the person. |

It is important to be sensitive to each person's feelings. Children should be taught to choose an appropriate time and place for discussing difficult topics. For example, a child should not tell his or her mother about a note from the teacher when she is just walking in the door from work. Children can be taught to ask, "Is this a good time to talk?"

Children should be taught to use caring language as a part of their communication even when they are angry. Caring language is nonthreatening and lets people know that you respect them. Suggestions for using caring language include: use the person's name; tell how you feel; identify the problem; tell what you want done; and learn to say, "I apologize" when it is appropriate.

Fighting fair works because it keeps the doors of communication open, attacks problems not people, helps people take responsibility for their behavior, and heals hurt feelings. Steps to teaching children how to fight fair include:

- *Identifying the problem.* Some helpful questions to ask include "What is really bothering you?", "What do you want?" and "What does the other person want?" Let each person involved state the problem from his or her own point of view.

- *Focusing on the problem.* Conflicts can have many traps. If the other person uses a foul, be careful not to get hooked on the bait. When the child yells, "Don't blame me! I didn't do it!" remember to focus on the problem. A sarcastic response only keeps the conflict alive. An effective response is, "Well, the problem is that we have toys all over the family room, and we need to put them away so we will know where they are when we want to play with them."

- *Attacking the problem, not the person.* Caring language opens the lines of communication. Fouls put people on the defensive: "Jimmy, I'm sorry I pushed you in the cafeteria line. I was really angry because I heard you talking about me to Joe. I'd rather work on us getting along than spending time trying to hurt you."

- *Listening with an open mind.* Do not interrupt the other person, do not put words in the other person's mouth, use a non-threatening tone of voice, ask questions when you are not clear, and allow for disagreement.

- *Treating the person's feelings with respect.* Two statements that communicate respect are: "You seem angry. Do you want to talk about it?" and "I care about how you are feeling now."

- *Taking responsibility for your actions.* Blaming others avoids taking responsibility. Ask, "What can I do to handle this problem?"

## Indicators/Measures of Success

When children feel that they must fight, and they use the techniques listed above, this intervention can be considered successful.

## Forms

Fighting Fair Flash Cards, pages 198-199.

## Suggested Readings and Resources

Drew, N. *Learning the Skills of Peacemaking.* Rolling Hills Estates, CA: Jalmar, 1987.

Kreidler, W. *Creative Conflict Resolution.* Glenview, IL: Scott, Foresman & Co., 1984.

Schmidt, F., and A. Friedman. *Fighting Fair for Families.* Miami Beach: Peace Education Foundation, 1994.

# Filial Therapy

## When to Use the Technique

Filial therapy is used with children who have emotional problems, behavior problems, developmental difficulties, and certain physical handicaps.

## Patient Age and Profile

Filial therapy is recommended for use with children from infancy through 12 years old.

## How the Technique Works

In filial therapy, parents are taught to use the technique of client-centered play therapy, developed by Virginia Axline in the 1940s. In client-centered play therapy, the child guides and directs the play, while the adult follows the child's lead. A few rules are set for the play therapy session, and the child is gently but firmly stopped if the limits are crossed. Limits are set about hurting oneself or others, and about destruction of property. Other than that, the child is allowed to play as he or she desires. Limits are not placed on what the child is allowed to say.

In the sessions, the parent and child play in an environment where judgment and directives from the parent are momentarily suspended. The sessions take place weekly for a half hour at a time. The sessions are regularly scheduled, and each child gets his or her own session. If there are two parents, each parent will take a turn with the child every other week. The goal of the sessions is to help children become aware of feelings they have not allowed themselves to recognize. They learn to communicate their feelings through play, and the parent shows acceptance in order to help them cope with their feelings and emotional struggles.

The basic filial therapy program, as outlined by Ginsberg (1989), is as follows:

*Session 1.* Introduction and development of the relationship between the therapist and the family. The presenting problem is explored, and the entire family is observed playing together. The therapist gives the family feedback and a basic explanation of filial therapy.

### Definition

Filial therapy assumes that the child's interactions with his or her parents strongly affects the child's development. The technique trains parents to interact with the child in the same therapeutic manner that a therapist is trained, giving the child an optimal environment in which to develop.

*Session 2.* The first session is reviewed, and the benefits of the approach are elaborated upon by the therapist. The therapist models with each child while the parents observe.

*Session 3.* The therapist models with each child again while the parents observe. Some attention is paid to understanding each child's development and method of self-expression. The therapist reviews the play therapy guidelines with the parents so that they are ready to begin themselves in the next session.

*Session 4.* Each parent plays with a child according to the client-centered play therapy guidelines while the therapist observes. The therapist then provides the family with feedback and helps them to improve their play therapy skills.

*Session 5.* The parents again play individually with each child for 15 minutes under therapist supervision. At the end of the session, the purchase of toys is discussed along with ways to structure the home for the weekly sessions.

*Session 6.* Parents again play individually with each child while the therapist observes. The rest of the session is dedicated to discussion about organizing and structuring the home play session. The parents conduct the first home play session between the 6th and 7th session.

*Session 7.* The home play session is reviewed and the therapist provides further structure and supervision for the home sessions. Parents again have a home play session in the week between the 7th and 8th sessions.

*Session 8.* The home session is reviewed and any questions or problems are cleared up. The therapist suggests that the family come to the office less frequently at this point, perhaps every 2 to 4 weeks.

*Session 9.* The play sessions held in the intervening weeks are reviewed. Any changes that have occurred are examined at this time, and an evaluation is done regarding further treatment. If no other problems or areas of concern are identified, a session is set for three months later.

*Session 10.* The therapist again observes the parents playing with each child. Changes in the children are noted. Followup contact is set for an agreed-upon point in the near future, usually at least two weeks away and not more than a few months.

## Indicators/Measures of Success

As children begin to feel better about themselves, they will start to demonstrate mastery over their internal and external environment. This will result in both emotional and behavioral changes that may alleviate the presenting symptom.

## Suggested Readings and Resources

Guerney, B., L. Guerney, and M. Andronico. "Filial Therapy." *Yale Scientific Magazine,* 40, 6-14, 1966.

Guerney, L., L. Stover, and B. Guerney. *Training Manual for Parents: Instructions in Filial Therapy.* Mimeograph, Pennsylvania State College, 1972.

Ginsberg, B. "Training Parents as Therapeutic Agents with Foster/Adoptive Children Using the Filial Approach." *Handbook of Parent Training: Parents as Co-Therapists for Children's Behavior Problems.* New York: John Wiley & Sons, 1989.

Technique

# Find the Exception

## When to Use the Technique

All types of problems can be helped with this technique.

## Patient Age and Profile

This technique can be useful with any patient at any age. Behavioral research has shown that even children with persistent and chronic problems do not exhibit these problems all of the time. Behaviors tend to occur in "chunks" and at specific times, but they are perceived as happening "all of the time." Focusing on when the problem does not occur brings a new hopefulness to solving the problem and puts it in perspective. From a behavioral viewpoint, the therapist can also analyze the antecedents and consequences that occur during the time periods that are identified as "exceptions."

## How the Technique Works

Identifying exceptions to the problem opens up a window to finding a solution and a first step in therapy. For example, if the teenager is compliant just once a week, such as when getting an allowance, can a reward system be set up so that the teen gets part of the allowance every day?

## Indicators/Measures of Success

This technique can be measured formally with symptom checklists or informally as an ongoing part of therapy. For example, the child or family could be asked to draw the problem in some symbolic way at the beginning of each session, listing the things that have been successful in "shrinking it." If the problem has gotten "bigger" since the previous session, the session should focus on containing it and finding ways to shrink it for the next session.

## Suggested Readings and Resources

de Shazer, S. *Keys to Solutions in Brief Therapy.* New York: W. W. Norton, 1985.

---

### Definition

This technique is considered a "classic" element of solution-focused therapy. It is a type of reframing, which directs children and their families to see the positive rather than the negative aspects of a child's life. The people attending the therapy session are asked to identify times that are "exceptions" to the problem. For example, if parents describe their teenager as being "willful and stubborn all of the time," the therapist would ask the parents to "identify a time when he has been cooperative and compliant, even for a very short period of time."

---

# Genograms

## When to Use the Technique

Devised by family therapist Murray Bowen, this technique began as an investigative method for the therapist's increased understanding and recordkeeping. Therapists who keep this chart of a family's history can often refer to it or show the family its emerging patterns. Ideally this is a method of gathering and organizing family records and keeps the therapist from missing potentially relevant information. For example, a family brings in a young, anxious, overprotected child. The genogram reveals an unusual number of deaths of young children in the family for over two generations. This context provides an important clue for understanding the child's symptoms and the parents' tendancy to overprotect.

## Patient Age and Profile

This technique is clearly for adults rather than for children, because children rarely have the kind of information required for a genogram. It is probably better used by families with the intellectual skills and curiosity to make the maximum number of connections.

## How the Technique Works

By having a pictorial record of three generations, with names, dates, relationships, sibling positions, marital status, and so on, a family tree is constructed for all to witness. Families may possibly see patterns of emotional interconnectedness that they had previously overlooked. Family systems theorists have demonstrated that family emotional patterns tend to repeat themselves over generations; the same unresolved emotional issues can be handed down like legacies.

Hypotheses may be constructed and tested on issues of closeness, overall emotional functioning, sibling rivalry, and so on, with the data so clearly drawn. When evaluated information is represented in a genogram, the therapist and family together are better able to understand the hidden emotional forces connecting generations.

## Indicators/Measures of Success

As an assessment tool there can be no question of success. Whether the data thus obtained is useful for the family members to extricate

> ### Definition
>
> A family genogram is a way to record the patterns and influences of three generations of a family. It is a graphic aid or "map" of the history of the family that allows therapist and patients alike to view pictorially family patterns and connections. A genogram is constructed like a family tree, using squares for males and circles for females; lines show marriage and kinship. Deaths, divorces, ages, and any other pertinent information is included.

themselves from presented patterns is another issue. But genograms may light the way, and sometimes families may see things that enable them to change old, difficult scenarios.

## Suggested Readings and Resources

Ivey, A., M. Ivey, and L. Simek-Morgan. *Counseling and Psychotherapy: A Multicultural Perspective.* Needham Heights, MA: Allyn & Bacon, 1997.

# Gestalt Therapy

## When to Use the Technique

Gestalt therapy is very useful with angry or traumatized children.

## Patient Age and Profile

Young children of school age and adolescents can benefit most from this technique.

## How the Technique Works

Gestalt therapy sees repressed conflicts as inflicting a cost on the entire person. The therapy aims to increase awareness of what the person needs at the moment.

This approach can be particularly helpful with angry children because it considers excursions into the past irrelevant; the focus is on the "here and now," on what is said as much as on nonverbal clues to hidden feelings.

Some common methods used in Gestalt therapy are role-playing, exaggeration of symptoms or behavior, use of fantasy, the principle of staying with the immediate moment, the use of the word "I" rather than "it" as a way to assume responsibility for behavior, learning how to talk to rather than at someone, becoming aware of bodily senses, and learning to "stay with feelings" until they are understood and integrated.

Gestalt therapy with children most often employs a specific process consisting of the following components:

- *Developing the relationship.* In working with children, the relationship is the foundation of the therapeutic process.

- *Evaluating and establishing contact.* The therapist comes into contact with the child to establish the "I/Thou" relationship. With troubled children, the focus of therapy is to help the child maintain contact—"to bring the self fully to the session."

- *Strengthening the child's sense of self and self-support.* Children, especially those who have experienced trauma, need self-support to express

---

### Definition

Developed by Fritz Perls and based on the principles of Gestalt psychology, Gestalt therapy focuses on all aspects of the person: senses, body, emotions, and intellect. It teaches that the child's developing sense of self leads to positive contact with his or her environment and the people in it. As each need surfaces and is met without hindrance, not only does the child achieve homeostasis and balance, but he or she also gains new levels of growth and development.

blocked emotions. Experiences with seeing, hearing, touching, tasting, and smelling can focus new awareness on one's senses.

- *Encouraging emotional expression.* Disturbed children are confused by the aggressive energy required to take action. They either push it down or express themselves through aggressive action. To help children express their feelings, this therapy uses creative, expressive, and projective techniques (such as drawing, painting, fantasy and imagery, storytelling, puppetry, sand play, dramatics, music, metaphors, body movement, sensory awareness, and so on) that can evoke strong feelings.

- *Helping the child learn to nurture the self.* This involves helping the child learn to accept the disliked parts of himself or herself and to work toward feelings of integration and self-worth.

- *Focusing on the child's process, particularly aspects of his or her way of being in the world that may be inappropriate.* The symptoms and behaviors that bring a child to therapy manifest themselves in the way he or she copes and survives in a stressful world. When a child moves through the therapeutic process, these behaviors basically drop away, and the child evidences a much more healthful mode of living and interacting.

- *Finalizing the therapy.* Closure is not just a mere ending but a vital component of the Gestalt therapy process. However, closure must be seen in a developmental context; children are only capable of working through situations at their particular developmental level.

One of many Gestalt therapy techniques for dramatizing a child's feelings is to have the child sit in different chairs to play the various "parts" of himself or herself—a guilty conscience, a resentful but submissive trait, and so on. The therapist helps the child bring these parts into harmony by making them blatantly obvious, and the anticipated outcome is that the integration of the fragmented parts helps the child work out anger and become self-reliant.

The chair "props" include the "hot-seat," a chair for the child who chooses to "work," and an empty chair facing the child onto which the child projects his or her many selves.

An angry child who, according to Gestalt psychology, is aware of only one "pole" (the angry and aggressive one), can develop an awareness of his or her fragmented parts by starting a dialog and acting out various roles, switching chairs in each role. The "hot seat" would be the angry self; the empty chair is for the other parts of the self.

The use of the hot-seat for role-playing with angry children can be very effective. The child imagines another person in the opposite chair and speaks to this person, saying what's really on his or her mind. The child then becomes the other and responds. The root of a child's anger can come to the surface in this manner, and it can be understood and resolved.

## Indicators/Measures of Success

The idea behind Gestalt therapy is that by being aware of one's feelings and directly encountering them, one can change. When this is achieved, this form of therapy can be considered effective.

## Suggested Readings and Resources

Engler, J., and D. Goleman. *The Consumer's Guide to Psychotherapy.* New York: Simon & Shuster, 1992.

James, M., and D. Jongeward. *Born to Win: Transactional Analysis with Gestalt Experiments.* Reading, MA: Addison-Wesley, 1971.

Kottman, T., and C. Schaefer, eds. *Play Therapy in Action.* Northvale, NJ: Jason Aronson, 1993.

O'Connor, K., and C. Schaefer, eds. *Handbook of Play Therapy, Volume Two: Advances and Innovations.* New York: Wiley, 1994.

Technique

# Humor and Banter

## When to Use the Technique

Since laughter is the best medicine, banter may engage resistant children who otherwise attempt to block out the therapist and the message. With depressed, disabled, or sensitive clients it is of utmost importance that they not feel that the counselor is making fun of them or laughing at them.

## Patient Age and Profile

Silly, nonsensical behavior can be a tool for reaching very young children. Teaching older children to be able to laugh at potential difficulties can help them find alternative solutions. The most important issue here is the quality of the relationship between the client and counselor. A good rapport is crucial to using this approach.

## How the Technique Works

Laughter and humor have been linked with healing in both ancient wisdom and modern science. As therapists it is all too easy for us to become grim and humorless in our pursuit of mental health for our clients. A lighter approach can help us prevent burnout as well as potentially engage stubborn children and provide a new and unthreatening way of seeing things. In order to use this approach effectively, the therapist obviously needs a good sense of humor and one that may be turned inward as well as on others. In other words, it is important not to take ourselves too seriously if we are using humor therapeutically.

## Indicators/Measures of Success

If the patient is able to laugh or even smile at an interaction, then it is likely there has been some utility in this interchange. If the patient begins to tell jokes or bring up the humor when he or she sees it, then the success of generalization to other situations has occurred. If the patient withdraws or becomes less trusting, or is in any way hurt by this technique, then it should be discontinued.

### Definition

Humor and banter, although not specific techniques, describe an approach to interaction with clients. In this approach the therapist may deliberately make humorous comments in order to ease a tense moment or to bring about a change. The therapist may exaggerate aspects of an individual's or family's dysfunctional behavior. Like reframing, humor "relaxes" the situation so that new possibilities may arise.

## Suggested Readings and Resources

Farrelly, F., and J. Brandsma. *Provocative Therapy*. Cupertino, CA: Meta Publications, 1974.

Fry, W., and W. Salameh. *Handbook of Humor and Psychotherapy*. Sarasota, FL: Professional Resource Exchange, 1987.

Kuhlman, T. *Humor and Psychotherapy*. Homewood, IL: Dow Jones-Irwin, 1984.

Technique

# Hypnotherapy

## When to Use the Technique

Hypnosis is used in conjunction with psychotherapy to treat anxiety disorders, stress, and chronic pain, among other problems.

## Patient Age and Profile

Hypnotherapy has been used with children as young as 3 and 4 years old. Some therapists believe that the suggestibility and visual imagination of young children make them ideal candidates for hypnotherapy. Self-hypnosis can be taught to children ages 8 and up.

## How the Technique Works

Hypnosis is used with psychotherapy in order to utilize the resources of the unconscious mind. When a client has tried unsuccessfully to consciously change, it may be easier to affect change unconsciously. According to Yapko (1990), the stages of hypnotic interaction are: (1) rapport building and attentional absorption, (2) trance induction and intensification, (3) trance utilization (therapy), and (4) disengagement and reorientation.

In the first phase, the child needs to narrow his or her focus to include only the clinician and the issue at hand. The therapist should discuss with the child the goals of the treatment and assess the child's responsiveness. The clinician uses this time to determine how to move the course of therapy along in accordance with the stated goals.

In the trance induction phase, the clinician provides something specific for the child to focus on. The child's conscious mind is occupied, which allows it to dissociate from the unconscious mind. The greater the degree of dissociation obtained, the deeper the trance will be. The trance induction phase also sets up the pattern of the child responding to the guidance of the clinician. The clinician can induce the trance using progressive muscle relaxation, eye fixation techniques, counting methods, or any number of other techniques. In general, anything that focuses the child's attention and promotes a feeling of comfort and well-being can be used to induce a trance.

### Definition

Hypnotherapy is a technique in which the client, with the help of the therapist, reaches a state of deep relaxation, referred to as a trance or altered state of consciousness, where it is assumed that he or she can be guided to utilize the resources of the unconscious in resolving conflicts. In children, hypnotherapy has generally been used as a means to help gain control over extreme emotional states, such as phobias or anxieties, as well as with physical problems, such as pain control. Traditional, or "trance," hypnotherapy is distinguished from Ericksonian hypnotherapy, where suggestions are often given to the client in a state of "paradoxical confusion," which does not involve prior relaxation training.

To therapeutically utilize the trance, the therapist can choose from a number of different techniques. One such technique is called "changing personal history." This is used when an incident in the client's life has led to some sort of a negative pattern. For example, if a child was sexually abused by a teacher, he or she might believe that all teachers are harmful and develop a school phobia as a result. Using the changing personal history technique, the clinician takes the child back to the incident and recreates it, this time with the appropriate support and intervention that was missing from the real incident.

When the therapeutic work is done, the therapist should gently bring the child out of the trance. If the child does not immediately come out of the trance, he or she is instructed to take whatever time is needed and come out of the trance when ready. As a trance is simply strongly focused attention, it is impossible for the child to get "stuck" in the trance.

Deep relaxation is also associated with other techniques, including biofeedback, meditation, and progressive relaxation.

## Indicators/Measures of Success

Generally the client will report whether the technique has been successful or progress was made.

## Suggested Readings and Resources

Yapko, M. *Trancework: An Introduction to the Practice of Clinical Hypnosis*. New York: Brunner/Mazel, 1990.

# The Imaginary Time Machine

## When to Use the Technique

This technique can be used with just about any type of emotional or behavioral problem.

## Patient Age and Profile

Children of all ages and all family members can be taught this technique.

## How the Technique Works

This technique is derived from solutions-oriented therapy and strategic family therapy. Its therapeutic intentions are to give the child or family a sense that life can be "conflict-free," to anticipate that life in the future can be without problems, to allow the child the opportunity to go back in time and remember past successes and coping strategies, and to enjoy in fantasy what one does not immediately have in reality.

The technique can be used at any stage of treatment. It is particularly useful when a therapist is "stuck," because it can propel the treatment forward. It can also be used as a family assignment, with the additional directions, "Write a story or draw a picture about your trip."

## Indicators/Measures of Success

If this technique is effective it should be pleasurable to the child or family, and signs of this enjoyment should be evident to the therapist.

## Suggested Readings and Resources

Selekman, M. *Solution-Focused Therapy with Children.* New York: Guilford Press, 1997.

---

### Definition

This technique asks the child to imagine how things might be in the future or might have been in the past. It allows children (and families) to take a "vacation" from their problems and experience a time that is conflict-free.

---

# The Imaginary Feelings X-Ray Machine

## When to Use the Technique

This technique is most useful for children with internalized disorders, such as depression, anxiety, or fears. It works equally well in individual, group, or family settings.

## Patient Age and Profile

This technique would work best with children old enough to discuss their feelings (5+) and young enough to not think that the exercise is "babyish." In a group counseling situation where rapport and trust have already been established, it can be used with older children and teenagers as well.

## How the Technique Works

Children find this family art task to be fun and tend to become more aware of their emotions through it. Family members also tend to be surprised when they visually discover the child's feelings about himself or herself and the family situation.

## Indicators/Measures of Success

The benefits of this technique can be measured informally by observing the patient's reaction to the technique, or more formally by a standardized symptom checklist.

## Suggested Readings and Resources

Selekman, M. *Solution-Focused Therapy with Children.* New York: Guilford Press, 1997.

### Definition

This art-therapy technique is described by Selekman (1997) but has been used in many different forms by art therapists. The child is asked to lie down on a large piece of paper, and the counselor draws his or her outline. Then the child is told to pretend that there is an "imaginary X-ray machine" that will show the feelings that he or she has inside. A box of crayons and markers is given to the child to draw those feelings. Once the picture is completed, it is discussed with the child.

Technique

# Implosion Therapy

## How the Technique Works

In this technique, the child is exposed to the anxiety-producing stimuli either in a real-life situation or in fantasy. It is assumed that overexposure to a harmless feared stimulus will desensitize the child to that stimulus. It should be noted that implosion differs from systematic desensitization, which is a more gradual exposure to a stimulus, and that sudden and extreme exposure is considered an aversive technique by many therapists.

## When to Use the Technique

This technique is generally used with fears, phobias, and other anxious responses.

## Patient Age and Profile

This technique is generally used with children over the age of 10. Because it is aversive in nature, it is important to have a good understanding of the technique before using it.

## Indicators/Measures of Success

A self-report rating scale, establishing a baseline and measuring anxiety/fear immediately after the session as well as in context, is the best way to measure the success of the technique.

## Suggested Readings and Resources

Ollendick, T. *Clinical Behavior Therapy with Children*. New York: Plenum Press, 1981.

---

### Definition

Implosion therapy is a behavior-modification technique often used to counteract phobias, fears, and other anxious responses in children. The child is exposed for a prolonged period of time to the specific anxiety-producing stimulus that is being targeted. As the child is exposed to the stimulus and feels the accompanying anxiety without coming to harm, the anxiety response can be unlearned and a more appropriate response invoked.

# Kindness Diary

The children should be instructed to keep a Kindness Diary. Ask them to do one small, kind thing each day (such as holding a door open for someone or sending a get well card) and spend one hour each week helping others. Record the activity on a daily basis and discuss the children's reaction to what happened. Reinforce all positive thoughts, feelings, and actions.

## When to Use the Technique

All children will benefit from this type of program, but it may be particularly helpful to children with antisocial behavior problems. Generally speaking, it is easier to teach a new behavior than to modify an existing one, so that teaching prosocial behavior in small steps may be the most effective route to behavioral change.

## Patient Age and Profile

Children ages 3 to 12 will benefit from this intervention.

## How the Technique Works

Emotions, thoughts, and behaviors are all linked together. If you change one, it is almost inevitable that you will change the others as well. Teaching children to behave more kindly and considerately has many rewards. It engenders nurturing and caring feelings, improves self-worth and self-confidence, teaches important social skills, and makes other people think more favorably toward children with behavior problems.

## Indicators/Measures of Success

If a Kindness Diary is kept on a regular basis, then this in itself is a measure of success. It serves as an anecdotal recording of behavioral change.

## Suggested Readings and Resources

Conari Press Editors. *Kids' Random Acts of Kindness.* Berkeley, CA: Conari Press, 1994.

---

**Definition**

The first step in creating a "Kindness Diary" involves telling children about the random acts of kindness movement, namely that doing even very small acts of kindness can change the lives of others. The therapist (or parents) can give examples from their own lives or read stories of the effects of kindness.

# The Life-Space Interview

## When to Use the Technique

This technique is particularly useful in working with children who have significant or chronic emotional problems, including acting-out behaviors, tantrums, and emotional and aggressive outbursts. The life-space interview is also helpful in milieu therapy as practiced in special classes for emotionally troubled children or in residential settings.

## Patient Age and Profile

Older children, who can become cognizant of insights into their problems, can be helped by this technique.

## How the Technique Works

This technique is extremely effective in working with angry children because it gives parents, teachers, or child-care workers a consistent way to address volatile emotional outbursts. In providing consistency and structure, the child will begin to feel "safe" in expressing his or her feelings and will develop a more trusting relationship with the adults who are trying to help.

The intervention operates on two levels: It provides emotional first-aid, and it helps the child gain insight into chronic, self-defeating emotional and behavioral patterns. Whether or not the adult wishes to go to the second level of the intervention will depend on a number of factors.

Staff and parents should decide together what issue is particularly relevant at the present time, and focus on that issue as appropriate opportunities arise. The issue on which the staff focuses their efforts should be one that is not so deeply "repressed" as to render it unavailable to the child.

The role of the adult conducting the interview should be considered; a person seen as a friend is less likely to be effective in a situation likely to call up hostile feelings in the child. An authority figure may be better able to absorb some of these feelings.

Be aware of both the adult's and the child's emotional limits at the time the incident occurred. Don't start something that neither the adult nor the child can properly finish. On the other hand, too much first-aid can result in the child becoming dependent upon others to calm him or her; a careful balance must be struck. Be aware also of what impact the immediate surroundings may be having on the child and his or her defenses when making interpretations or offering support.

Timing can be crucial; although you don't want to lose the impact of the event's proximity, sometimes it is better to wait a short while to allow some of the initial burst of aggressive feeling to dissipate.

Using standard therapeutic techniques such as reflecting, naming feelings, observations, and interpretations, the caregiver can accomplish many objectives related to the overall goals of providing support or creating an opportunity for insight. These have been articulated by Fritz Redl (1966) in his original description of this technique and will be briefly mentioned here.

In providing emotional first-aid at a time of crisis, the caregiver may do one or more of the following:

- *Drain off frustration.* This refers to the need to support the child in expressing his or her legitimate anger and frustration. It is a way to help the child to verbalize rather than act out feelings and insures that this frustration won't be added to the angry child's already long list of previous insults.

- *Help the child manage feelings of panic, fury, and guilt.* The angry child is often immature in his or her ability to process and release strong negative feelings. The adult who stays with him or her must remain calm in order to provide both a model and a container for these emotions. As the child settles down, talking with him or her about alternatives will increase problem-solving skills.

- *Maintain lines of communication.* Sometimes at a time of crisis, when the child is in a rage, it is important to continue some form of communication in order to prevent the child's relationship with the caregiver from breaking down altogether. Talk about anything nonthreatening at the moment. Remind the child of any rules that pertain to the place where the emotional outburst occurred and the consequences of breaking them. This is a means of increasing the child's ability to think ahead and delay impulsive acts.

- *Act as an "umpire" for the child's emotional choices.* The caregiver focuses on helping the child recognize the choices that must be made between the desire to express immediate needs and impulses or dealing with feelings in a more positive way.

In taking advantage of the emotional outburst to increase the child's insight into his or her behaviors, the caregiver should:

- *Provide a reality check.* The angry, aggressive child often displays a distorted perception of others' intentions and responses. At the time of an incident, the caregiver should gently but firmly go over the problem, point out these distortions, and reinterpret the situation for the child.

- *Confront secondary gains.* Although angry and aggressive behavior seems on the surface to be self-defeating, it almost always has "secondary gains" for the child (i.e., on an unconscious level the child feels the behavior satisfies some need). Some incidents provide an opportunity to explore with the child whether the gains are worth the price.

- *Increase awareness of underlying values and needs.* The angry child has difficulty admitting that he or she needs love and tenderness. Nevertheless, during an outburst, adults may lay the ground-work for later discussion of more difficult underlying concerns and needs.

- *Suggest alternative responses.* The crisis provides an opportunity to model and discuss alternative responses to stressful events. Supporting the child when he or she chooses a positive alternative can also be helpful.

## Indicators/Measures of Success

Using the above techniques, the caregiver attempts to use a fleeting life experience to further long-range therapeutic goals. When the child begins to feel safe in expressing feelings and develops a more trusting relationship with the adults who are trying to help, this intervention will have been successful.

## Suggested Readings and Resources

Johnson, J., W. Rosbury, and L. Siegel. *Approaches to Child Treatment.* New York: Pergamon Press., 1986.

Redl, F. *When We Deal With Children.* New York: The Free Press, 1966.

# Mentoring

## When to Use the Technique

Mentoring seems to be particularly helpful for aggressive or high-risk children and teens.

## Patient Age and Profile

Mentors are typically used with children 10 and older who do not have appropriate role models in their lives.

## How the Technique Works

Mentoring works largely because of the behavioral principle of modeling. On the most basic level, just spending time with a troubled child or teenager appears to engender a sense of trust and an increased motivation to achieve.

## Indicators/Measures of Success

The success of mentoring programs is usually measured by informal means, such as better grades, less absenteeism in school, and anecdotal assessment.

## Forms

The Mentoring Contract, page 203.

## Suggested Readings and Resources

www.mentoring.org ("One to One"). The National Mentoring Partnership (on-line resource)

### Definition

Mentoring involves finding older role models for children or teens, who will spend time doing productive activities with them. Programs such as Big Brothers and Big Sisters have shown the effectiveness of pairing high-risk children with role-models. Studies have shown that these programs are effective in reducing school drop-out, drug involvement, and antisocial behaviors.

Technique

# Mind Mapping

## When to Use the Technique

This technique can be applied to any problem that can benefit from creative problem-solving strategies.

## Patient Age and Profile

Children over 7 and their families can benefit from this technique.

## How the Technique Works

Studies have suggested that most people find it much easier to understand a visual representation of the problem than a verbal description. Research on note-taking skills show that the best note takers record key words in a clear and organized manner. The Gestalt theory suggests that learning and change are facilitated by understanding the "whole" of a problem, identifying each of the individual parts, and seeing how the different parts fit together. Selekman (1997) suggests counselors can help visualize a family's problems by the following four steps:

1. In the center of a piece of paper, draw a symbol or picture of the problem that represents the child's or the family's complaints.

2. Write down the key words used by the child or family to describe the problem.

3. Connect the key words radiating out from the problem.

4. Use color coding or pictures to help describe how key issues are related.

Pictograms, or "mind-maps," can also be useful for the child or family, to help conceptualize the problem and point to potential places where the problem can be changed. Directions for a family or client might be:

*Draw a picture of your problem in the center of a page.*

*In a circle around the original problem, draw or write the main things you think contribute to your problem.*

*Connect the contributing factors that are related by drawing lines between them.*

### Definition

Mind mapping is a way of visualizing the problem and its salient features. Getting a concrete picture of a problem can be a significant step forward in solving it. This technique helps concretize vague or unclear issues and will potentially help point the way toward solutions.

*Now draw the picture again, with the factors that are related grouped together in and put in a box.*

*Is there anyway that things in the box can be worked on at the same time?*

## Indicators/Measures of Success

The mind-mapping technique can be used by clients as a way of recording therapeutic progress. Each session can begin by mapping what the problem currently is and end by mapping how the problem can be dealt with between sessions.

## Suggested Readings and Resources

Selekman, M. *Solution-Focused Therapy with Children.* New York: Guilford Press, 1997.

Technique

# The Miracle Question

## When to Use the Technique

Any problem that is causing family members to get "stuck" can be helped by this technique.

## Patient Age and Profile

Children over 10, families, and other people in the child's life can all be helped using this technique.

## How the Technique Works

This technique is a key part of solution-focused therapy. Its intent is to help reframe the problem and motivate people to see the potential solutions rather than be stuck in the complaints and conflicts that make up the problem.

Selekman (1997) advises the therapist to be patient and give family members plenty of time to think and respond to the miracle question. They should be told to pretend or to "play around" with the idea that all their problems are magically solved. The therapist should avoid asking leading questions and allow family members to introduce their own unique solutions and envisioned changes. Once they have shared their miracle pictures, the therapist can explore with them other changes they may have thought about that might actually be happening and ask whether any of their miracles are already beginning to happen.

Some followup questions might include:

- Who will be most affected by this miracle?
- Who will be most surprised?
- How will things be different in the short term (tomorrow)?
- How will things be affected in the long term (a year from now)?
- Who might be angry that this miracle happened?
- How will things be different in school?
- How will things be different with friends?

### Definition

This simple technique is used to help determine how much help a child's family or other people in the child's life will be in dealing with the referring problem. It begins with this statement: "What if a miracle happened tomorrow, and the problem that you are concerned about today suddenly disappeared?"

## Indicators/Measures of Success

Since this is a diagnostic technique, its effectiveness in stimulating change cannot specifically be measured, and in fact its direct measurement might work counter-therapeutically by refocusing the client on the problem. The "miracle" projected by the patient(s) before therapy might best be measured by a post-therapy satisfaction questionnaire.

## Suggested Readings and Resources

Selekman, M. *Solution-Focused Therapy with Children.* New York: Guilford Press, 1997.

# The Mutual Storytelling Technique

To begin the technique, the therapist asks the child to tell a story. Upon hearing it, the therapist determines the psychodynamic meaning of the story, and chooses one or two themes that appear to be important to the child. The therapist then tells a story of his or her own, using the same characters in a similar setting. Keeping the critical themes in mind, the therapist tailors this story to portray positive resolution of the situations originally described by the child. This allows the therapist to introduce to the child healthier ways of resolving conflicts.

The mutual storytelling technique was developed in the 1960s by Richard Gardner. He developed the technique as a way of communicating with children at their own level and found it to be useful for treating a wide range of disorders. He used the technique as a basis for several other "derivative" techniques, including the Bag of Words (stories told in response to picking a word at random from a small bag); the Bag of Toys (stories told using small toys as a starting-off point); and the Bag of Faces (stories told based upon photographs of faces showing different expressions). Dr. Gardner has also published two games based on this technique, "The Pick and Tell Game" and "The Storytelling Card Game."

### When to Use the Technique

This technique has been used for many different types of disorders. However, it should only be used with children who are otherwise incapable of analyzing the stories they tell.

### Patient Age and Profile

This technique is used with children who will tell stories but who are unwilling to analyze them. Children who are willing to analyze their own stories should be encouraged to do so. This technique is used as a supplement to other forms of treatment, rather than as a treatment on its own.

### How the Technique Works

This technique was originally developed by Gardner as a way to help "resistant" children verbalize and communicate with the therapist. It is

## Definition

In the mutual storytelling technique, the therapist and child exchange stories, with the therapist providing corrective and positive modeling stories. Through the use of these stories, the therapist speaks the child's language and talks at a level understandable to the child.

presumed that the metaphors revealed by the child's stories are indicators of unconscious processes, much like projective techniques. It is further assumed that the therapist's stories will be understood on a metaphoric level and through modeling will have an influence on the child's stories. In other words, the child's unrealistic, self-defeating, or dysfunctional views of himself or herself or the world will be modified by the therapist's offerings. The stories can also be used as a jumping-off point to develop insight about the child's conflicts or behaviors and as a way to enhance the therapeutic relationship.

## Indicators/Measures of Success

The success of this or other storytelling techniques must be judged in terms of symptom alleviation and a reduction in the behaviors that led to the referring problem.

## Suggested Readings and Resources

Gardner, R. *Psychological Interventions with Resistant Children* (audiotape). Cresskill, NJ: Creative Therapeutics.

Dr. Gardner's games and books can be ordered through Creative Therapeutics, Cresskill, NJ; 800/544-6162.

Technique

# Negotiating

### Definition

Negotiating is a basic means of getting what you want from others. It is also a back-and-forth communication designed to reach an agreement with the other side, which has some shared interests and some opposing interests. The disputing parties communicate directly with each other to resolve the conflict peacefully, without coercion or aggression. Negotiation helps both parties to state their individual needs, focusing on their interests rather than their positions, and to generate options for mutual gain.

## When to Use the Technique

Aggressive and angry children can benefit most from this technique.

## Patient Age and Profile

Children of all ages, even very young ones, can be taught this skill, which will last a lifetime.

## How the Technique Works

In *Creating the Peaceable School*, Bodine, Crawford, and Schrumpf present steps for successful negotiation similar to those used in mediation. It should be noted here that negotiation is similar to mediation with the exception that it has no intermediary. With a teacher's assistance and encouragement, even very young students can learn the negotiation process and use it to solve problems. The authors pinpoint the following goals for the negotiator in a conflict:

- *The negotiator listens with empathy.* Effective communication skills are essential to successful negotiation. When emotions run high, the negotiator must be able to both acknowledge them and clarify perceptions, thus freeing the disputants to work on the problem. Specifically, the negotiator must attend to the problem, using nonverbal behaviors to indicate that the listener finds what the other party is thinking and feeling of interest and wants to understand; summarize or restate facts by repeating the most important points; and clarify by using open-ended questions and statements to obtain more information.

- *The negotiator suspends judgment.* The successful negotiator remains open and objective, and avoids justifying and arguing for a particular position but rather works to explain his or her interests.

- *The negotiator is respectful.* Being respectful involves working to understand the other person's emotions and beliefs. The successful negotiator is able to treat the other party fairly and without prejudice or disrespect. It also means honoring the other person's privacy by not spreading tales.

■ *The negotiator has a cooperative spirit.* This means that he or she allows others to satisfy their interests whenever possible without compromising his or her own interests. The successful negotiator views the negotiation process as being equal in importance to the problem's solution.

There are several clear steps that can lead to a successful negotiation. They include:

1. *Stating the problem.* The parties sit face to face and agree to take turns talking and listening. The facts are stated as both parties see them, without assigning blame but simply outlining what happened. Put-downs and name-calling have no place in negotiation; if tempers flare, the negotiations cannot be successful.

2. *Stating what you want and why.* This step involves ascertaining each person's point of view. One person talks, and the other listens. When the first person is finished, the other person summarizes what has been said. Then the order is reversed. Each person can add information or clarify what was said previously.

3. *Focusing on interests.* If interests are not disclosed, there is little chance of reaching an agreement that both sides can keep. Each party should say:

> I want _____ because _____.
>
> I want to solve the problem because _____.
>
> If this problem does not get solved, I _____.

4. *Create win-win options.* In this step, both parties attempt to advance several ideas that address the interests of both. Together, they should invent at least three possible options. This ensures that the "stronger" party will not intimidate the other. Both parties must cooperate in coming up with ideas that will mutually benefit them. Rules for brainstorming might include saying anything that comes to mind, refraining from judging ideas, and trying to think of unusual solutions.

5. *Evaluating options.* Negotiators work together as side-by-side problem-solvers to elaborate on or combine options to create new options. Then they evaluate each one by saying, "Is this option fair?" "Can we do it?" "Do we think it will work?"

6. *Creating an agreement.* A plan of action should be developed that will put the idea into effect, specifying who, what, where, when, and how.

Not every issue is negotiable. Negotiators should recognize the difference between negotiable and non-negotiable issues and learn to say "No" when someone tries to negotiate a non-negotiable issue.

## Indicators/Measures of Success

When disputing parties communicate directly with each other to resolve a conflict peacefully, without coercion or aggression, the negotiating process is successful.

## Suggested Readings and Resources

Bodine, R., D. Crawford, and F. Schrumpf. *Creating the Peaceable School*. Champaign, IL: Research Press, n.d.

Fisher, R., and W. Ury. *Getting to Yes*. New York: Penguin Books, n.d.

Kreidler, W. *Creative Conflict Resolution*. Glenview, IL: Scott, Foresman and Co., 1984.

Sadalla, G., M. Holmberg, and J. Halligan. *Conflict Resolution: An Elementary School Curriculum*. San Francisco: The Community Board Program, Inc.

# Neuro Linguistic Programming

NLP was originated by professor John Grinder and one of his students, Richard Bandler, at the University of California, Santa Cruz, in the 1970s. Grinder and Bandler drew from the works of Fritz Perls, Virginia Satir, and Milton Erickson.

The four principles of NLP include:

1. *Rapport.* This refers to the quality of the relationship one has with the self as well as with others. Mental rapport is established when different parts of the mind are united, physical rapport comes when a person's body parts are working well together, and spiritual rapport is manifested in a sense of belonging to something larger than one's individual identity. The first pillar of NLP is for the practitioner to first establish good rapport with himself or herself and then with other people.

2. *Goals and outcomes.* It is necessary to know what one wants in order to define success. NLP practitioners focus more on goals, outcomes, and success than they do on defining the problem. This creates a solution-focused atmosphere rather than a problem-focused one.

3. *Sensory acuity.* This means using one's five senses in order to tune in and get feedback about the self. A person may not be on course in terms of goals, but unless that person stops to look, listen, and feel long enough, he or she may continue, unaware, down the wrong path.

4. *Behavioral flexibility.* This means being aware of and choosing alternate options when indicated. Unfortunately it is easier for people to keep on attempting the same old solution even when it is clearly not working.

Researcher and NLP trainer Robert Dilts contributed to the field of NLP by conceptualizing logical levels—the different levels upon which relationships can be built:

*First level:* Environment (the when and where). This refers to the place people are in and the people they are interacting with. At this level, mutual history and shared circumstances build rapport. For example, a person who joins a special-interest club is likely to meet and build a rapport with other people with similar interests.

## Definition

Neuro linguistic programming (NLP) is a way of examining, understanding, and using verbal and nonverbal communication to promote therapeutic change. 'Neuro' refers to the mind, 'linguistic' refers to language, and 'programming' denotes behaviors and actions. As indicated by its name, NLP examines how people represent, understand, and process both their own behavior and that of others. By applying this understanding, the NLP practitioner can do such things as establish better rapport with a child or teach a child how to induce a specific feeling state at will.

*Second level:* Behavior (the what). In NLP, behavior includes thoughts and actions. This level encompasses a person's conscious actions.

*Third level:* Capability (the how). This refers to the level of skill the person has developed as a result of practice. Habits, thinking strategies, intrinsic skills, and learned skills are all part of this level.

*Fourth level:* Beliefs and values (the why). This refers to what a person believes is true and how much value he or she gives to a belief. Beliefs and values both limit and expand a person's horizons, and conflicting beliefs can coexist.

*Fifth level:* Identity (the who). This level speaks to a person's sense of self and the core values and beliefs that define that person. Although identity is difficult to change, it is possible to alter and expand it.

*Sixth level:* Spiritual. This is a person's connections to others as well as a sense of who that person is beyond personal identity. This could include participation in formal religion or a simple sense of being one with nature.

NLP provides the following ways of developing rapport and working effectively with children:

*Creating similarities.* In order to have a good rapport with children, it is necessary to establish some commonalities and similarities with them. This does not need to be done through style of dress, attitude, or language. Rather, rapport can be established by using the mirroring technique. To mirror the child, the adult chooses some aspect of the child's behavior to casually imitate. For example, if the child touches an ear, the adult does the same, and if the child breathes rapidly, the adult matches the pace. This needs to be done slowly and casually enough so that it is not noticed on a conscious level, or the child may feel like he or she is being mocked.

When this mirroring of behavior is done consistently, it is called pacing. Pacing creates the basis for all relationships; people tend to be most comfortable around other people who have similar behavior patterns. An adult can mirror and pace a child through breathing patterns, body movement, speech patterns, physical gestures, facial expressions and gestures, and the tempo, tonality, and volume of speech. Crossover mirroring is when the adult imitates a movement with a different body part than that used by the child, i.e., if the child moves a leg back and forth, the adult may move an arm back and forth in a similar movement.

***Leading and behavior change.*** After mirroring and pacing the student's behavior, it is possible to lead the child into new behavior patterns. When the adult is in sync with the child, the child will begin to respond to cues given off by the adult. To take advantage of this, the adult can imitate a hyperactive child's breathing, gradually slowing the pace down. The child should respond by slowing down also, thereby decreasing the hyperactive behavior.

***Representational systems.*** Each person has a preferred sensory base— either visual, auditory, kinesthetic, gustatory, or olfactory—through which he or she interprets the world. This preference is expressed through body movements, behavior, and language. For example, a child who says, "I see what you mean" processes information visually, while a child who says, "I heard what you said" processes things auditorially. The kinesthetic processor will use terms such as *hear, say,* and *listen;* the gustatory child will favor words such as *taste, sweet,* and *sour;* and the olfactory child will say words such as *smell, odor,* and *stink.* Once this preference has been identified, the adult can communicate with the child using that same modality. This allows for better rapport and more effective communication.

***Anchoring.*** This NLP technique helps a child to switch from one feeling state to another at will. For example, a child who gets anxious when sitting down to take a test can develop "anchors" that will trigger the feeling state associated with a more pleasant, relaxing memory. To do this, the child needs to be conditioned to experience the feelings when triggered to do so. A trigger such as pressure applied to the knuckle of a hand or grasping a wrist can be used. Nagel et al. (1985) describes how a teacher can help set up one of the triggers, or "anchors," as they are called in NLP:

1. Establish and maintain rapport with the student.

2. Ask the student to find a context or situation in which positive or good feelings such as joy, happiness, acceptance, success, etc., are or were felt.

3. Ask the student to relive that time or scene, and experience it in full detail by visualizing the experience. Tell the student to step inside his or her body and actually be there. Then instruct the student, "See what you see, hear what you hear, and feel what you feel. When you are really experiencing the event, slightly move your little finger and stay in the experience. (When doing this, use present tense verbs.)

4. When the teacher sees the student move the little finger, the teacher touches a "magic spot" (wrist, earlobe, etc.) and holds the spot for five seconds. The teacher then releases the touch. It is important that the

spot selected be both convenient and easily accessible to the student. This specific spot ultimately becomes the student's "magic button."

5. To test the anchor, have the student again touch the "magic button" to verify that it brings forth the same feelings. If the same positive feelings as experienced previously do not reoccur, repeat the above steps. Check to make sure you are touching the same spot with the same amount of pressure.

Once these anchors have been established, the child can trigger the desired feeling state at will. Several different responses can be established with different spots. For example, the child might want to have a spot to trigger relaxation, another one for confidence, and another one for success.

## When to Use the Technique

NLP is generally used to enhance and supplement therapy and other interactions. For example, a teacher would use the techniques with children in the classroom, or a parent could use the "magic button" technique with a child who is anxious about math.

## Patient Age and Profile

This technique has been used with school-age children of 6 but is most effective with older children (over age 10) and adolescents.

## How the Technique Works

NLP works off the theoretical assumption that the communication that generally occurs on a nonverbal, unconscious level can be made conscious. Doing so will benefit the person who, by becoming aware of the subtle communication, can then influence the interaction. For example, people who are communicating well tend to blink with the same frequency or have similar breathing patterns. This happens naturally when a good rapport has been established, but it can also be deliberately and consciously created.

## Indicators/Measures of Success

As a therapy system, NLP should be measured by instruments that can ascertain the alleviation of symptoms or client complaints.

## Suggested Readings and Resources

Nagel, C., et al. *Mega Teaching and Learning.* Portland, OR: Metamorphous Press, 1985.

O'Connor, J., and I. McDermott. *The Principle of NLP.* London: Thorsons, 1996.

# Nutrition Therapy

## When to Use the Technique

Food allergies have been associated with many different childhood disorders, including Attention Deficit and disruptive behavior disorders, tic disorders, elimination disorders, and depression. Allergies may cause symptoms that mimic a disorder, or they may exacerbate symptoms caused by a disorder.

## Patient Age and Profile

Nutrition therapy has been used successfully with people of all ages.

## How the Technique Works

Nutrition therapists hypothesize that a wide range of mental health symptoms may actually be caused by exposure to certain foods, affecting emotional and mental reactions along with physical ones. Changes in diet may also affect emotions even when no allergies exist. For example, appropriate levels of the biochemical serotonin are associated with an increased sense of well-being, and a low-sugar, low-fat diet has been known to increase the brain's ability to utilize serotonin.

There is also a belief that dietary supplements may be useful as an aid in treating certain childhood disorders. For example, small doses of melatonin, a naturally occurring biochemical synthesized from serotonin in the pineal gland, is being recommended to improve the sleep patterns of autistic children (Panksepp, 1991). It is hypothesized that autistic children with sleep problems may have brain disturbances that affect their sleep patterns, and that this over-the-counter sleep aid may promote better sleep, which in turn would lead to improved behavior and learning. It is widely accepted that different food items can cause irritability, aggressiveness, misbehavior, fatigue, hyperactivity, or depression; however, dietary considerations are rarely factored into a child's treatment plan. Foods cause biochemical reactions the way medications do, and at least hypothetically, changes in diet could be a substitute in some cases for psychotropic drugs.

## Indicators/Measures of Success

Changes in diet should cause behavioral change that can be measured by observational data collection or other behavioral measurement techniques.

### Definition

Nutrition therapy addresses the role that nutrition and food sensitivities/allergies have in affecting behavior, as well as how dietary changes or supplements can improve behavior.

## Suggested Readings and Resources

Crook, W. "Can What a Child Eats Make Him Dull, Stupid or Hyperactive?" *Journal of Learning Disabilities*, 13(5), 53-58, 1980.

Havard, J. "School Problems and Allergies." *Journal of Learning Disabilities,* 6(7), 27-29, 1973.

Panksepp, J., et al. "Naltrexone and Other Potential New Pharmacological Treatments of Autism." *Brain Dysfunction,* 4, 281-300, 1991.

Rapp, D. *Is This Your Child?* New York: William Morrow, 1991.

To find physicians who specialize in food/ecological sensitivities, you can contact the following:

The American Academy of Environmental Medicine
P. O. Box 16106
Denver, CO 80216

Pan-American Allergy Society
P. O. Box 947
Fredericksburg, TX 78624

To find allergy-free products, contact these agencies:

The Living Source
3500 MacArthur Drive
Waco, TX 76708
(817) 756-6341

Allergy Product Directory
P. O. Box 640
Menlo Park, CA 94026-0640
(415) 322-1663

# The Overcorrection Procedure

## Example

A defiant boy comes home from school, ignores his mother's greeting, throws his books and coat on the floor, and starts playing video games instead of doing his homework. Rather than punishing him for his rudeness with a time-out or loss of a privilege (which really doesn't teach him anything), his mother would instead meet him at the door, require him (and physically guide him if necessary) to put his things away, and then escort him to his room, where he would sit down to do his homework. But rather than just doing this once, he would have to do it as many as ten times (for up to twenty minutes), so as to rehearse this behavior until it is part of his behavioral repertoire.

In the positive practice stage, the adult not only explains how to behave but requires the child to actually perform and practice the proper behavior. In this way, there is no confusion in the child's mind as to how he or she is expected to behave in the future. The repeated practice of the desired behavior also helps the child remember it and perform it at a later date.

The restitution stage requires the child to restore the environment to a state that is as good as or better than that which existed before the inappropriate behavior took place. In this stage, the child learns that his or her inappropriate behavior directly affects others, and he or she must now work to "make things right."

In the above example, the child's inconsiderate and defiant behavior probably hurt his mother's feelings and certainly took time away from other important things that she might be doing. To provide restitution, the child might be required to write an apology note to his mother and to do a twenty-five minute chore (just slightly longer than the twenty minutes it took his mother to guide him in the positive practice phase).

The overcorrection technique was originally developed by Nathan Azrin and Richard Foxx, primarily for use with mentally retarded individuals. A survey of behavior modification in the early 1970s found that 20 percent of the behavioral programs used with this population included some form of overcorrection. The original intent of the authors was to present a technique that did not rely on severe punishments but rather

> ### Definition
>
> Overcorrection is a behavioral technique effective in reducing a wide range of inappropriate behaviors in children. The technique consists of two distinct stages: positive practice and restitution, which can be used either separately or together. Positive practice consists of having the child perform a behavior that is a positive alternative to the original misbehavior.

served to educate the client and make him or her accountable for problem behaviors. Although it continues to be used in many institutional settings, it has not caught on as a technique widely used by counselors and therapists, in spite of its effectiveness. This is probably due to the intensity of the technique, which often requires considerable time from an adult for its correct implementation as well as a direct confrontation with clients. The most widespread use of the technique is in initial toilet training of the two-and-a-half- to three-year-old, as detailed in Azrin's and Nunn's book *Toilet Training in a Day*. Their procedure actually toilet trains in four hours a child who is physiologically ready.

## When to Use the Technique

In reviewing the literature, this technique seems to be useful for an extremely broad spectrum of behaviors, including noncompliance, aggression, sharing, toileting, vandalism, swearing, stealing, improper eating habits, habit control, self-injurious behavior, and stereotyped behavior.

## Patient Age and Profile

Overcorrection has been used with a broad range of patient populations, from the severely retarded or autistic child to the non-handicapped population. This technique has been used with children as young as 2 for toilet training to adolescents and adults for habit control.

## How the Technique Works

Positive practice is primarily used when the "correct" behavior—the opposite of the one being targeted—does not occur frequently enough to be influenced by positive reinforcement. In many instances positive practice can also be used to inhibit the original behavior by competing with it. This is particularly true when the physical behavior does not seem to be in the conscious control of the client, such as with a habit, stereotyped behavior, or self-abusive behavior. The following are examples of positive practice with different instances of these behaviors:

- A boy slams the door when he is angry. He is made to close the door properly and calmly 10 times and then list 5 reasons why he is angry.

- A girl bites her nails. She is made to grasp and squeeze a tennis ball for 10 minutes.

- An institutionalized mentally handicapped child becomes agitated and disruptive. The client is required to go to bed for a period of time and lay quietly.

One of the most successful uses of positive practice has been called autism reversal (also termed functional movement training) and involves teaching the child outward-directed behaviors that are incompatible with the child's self-stimulatory reinforcing behavior. For example, a boy who engages in repetitive hand clapping is instructed to put his hands in his pockets or keep them together for five minutes. A girl who keeps moving her head back and forth is taught to press her head downward, tensing her neck in an isometric exercise. This type of exercise is usually preceded by a strong verbal reprimand and is always topographically appropriate—meaning that it involves the same body parts used in the self-stimulating or self-abusive behavior.

Restitutional acts should have the following characteristics:

1. They should be directly related to the misbehavior of concern.

2. They should immediately follow the disruptive action.

3. Their duration should be greatly extended beyond the completion of the first act.

Performance of restitutional acts should require very active participation and effort without pause, so as to immediately inhibit the original behavior. Restitution procedures designed for different classes of disruptive behaviors include:

*Household orderliness training for abuse of property.* Includes the remediation of the damage and improving the general appearance of the property. For example, a child who defiles cafeteria desks with graffiti would have to wash, clean, and polish all the tables in the cafeteria.

*Social reassurance training for psychological abuse to others.* Requires a verbal apology or some other way to show remorse. For example, a child who calls another one names might have to write a lengthy note of apology, demonstrating an understanding of why this is wrong.

*Oral hygiene training for biting people and chewing objects.* Requires the offender to brush his or her teeth with an antiseptic solution (i.e., Listerine). This has been used to eliminate thumb-sucking as well as biting.

*Medical assistance for physical abuse to others.* The offender must assist in cleansing and bandaging all wounds and in filling out a report of the incident.

In some instances positive practice and restitution are both used, such as in toilet training, where the child has to both practice going to the bathroom correctly (i.e., pulling pants down, sitting on the toilet, and trying to go to the bathroom) and also "restoring" things when there is an accident (i.e., rinsing out clothes, cleaning any soiled area, taking a bath or shower, etc.).

The overcorrection procedure can also include the following techniques:

*Awareness training.* In working on bad habits, clients are made to be more aware of their habits by describing the details of the movement to the counselor, using a mirror if necessary, while reenacting the movement several times.

*Response detection procedure.* In working with seemingly unconscious habits, such as tics, the client is taught to be aware of each instance of the habit either by the counselor alerting him or her or by the use of videotape.

*Early warning procedure.* The client is taught to recognize the earliest sign of a behavior or habit, such as when a nail biter first brings a hand toward the face.

*Social support procedures.* The family and close friends of the client are instructed to strengthen the client's motivation to change by: (1) commenting favorably when the behavior is not present; (2) reminding the child of the need to practice competing behaviors or habits; and (3) occasionally noting how improved things are when the behavior is under control. In addition, the counselor or therapist should periodically call or write to the client or otherwise reinforce the progress.

*Public display procedure.* When parents or teachers are wary about the child's ability to actually control a problem, they can watch a videotape of the client demonstrating the appropriate behavior in the counselor's office.

## Indicators/Measures of Success

The following are considered to be important prerequisites for the successful use of the overcorrection procedure.

1. It is necessary to have an adult available to do the overcorrection procedure with the child as soon as it happens. This might be a parent, a teacher, an aide, a residential worker, and so on.

2. The procedure must be consistently applied in an impartial and unemotional manner. No variation in the technique should occur except if reviewed and changed by a professional administering the program. If more than one person is administering the over-correction procedure, each must be adequately trained so that there is no variation in the way each one reacts.

3. Careful data must be kept on the administration and results of the program.

4. The overcorrection procedure can only be effective if the child already has the behavioral skills in his or her repertoire (although they are not being used). For example, if you are trying to a teach a 6-year-old child to stay in his seat for an entire reading period but he has never been able to sit in a group this long, it is unlikely that this technique will work.

5. Overcorrection should only be used for a few related misbehaviors at a time. It is important that the child is not overwhelmed by having the parent or therapist attempt to correct all misbehaviors at once.

6. Overcorrection is almost always used in conjunction with a positive reward program that reinforces the correct behavior. For example, if overcorrection were being used for stereotyped hand movements, the child should also be reinforced for appropriate play with toys, art materials, and so on.

## Suggested Readings and Resources

Axelrod, S., J. Brantner, and T. Meddock. "Overcorrection: A Review and Critical Analysis." *Journal of Special Education*, 12:4, 367-91, 1978.

Azrin, N., S. Kaplan, and R. Foxx. "Autism Reversal: Eliminating Stereotyped Self-stimulation of Retarded Individuals." *American Journal of Mental Deficiency*, 78:3, 241-48, 1973.

Azrin, N., and R. Nunn. "Habit Reversal: A Method of Eliminating Nervous Habits and Tics." *Behaviour Research and Therapy*, 11, 619-628, 1973.

Foxx, R., and N. Azrin. "Restitution: A Method of Eliminating Aggressive-disruptive Behavior of Retarded and Brain Damaged Patients." *Behaviour Research and Therapy*, 10, 15-27, 1972.

_____. "Dry Pants: A Rapid Method of Toilet Training Children." *Behaviour Research and Therapy*, 11, 435-42, 1973.

_____. "The Elimination of Autistic Self-Stimulatory Behavior by Overcorrection." *Journal of Applied Behavior Analysis*, 6, 1-14, 1973.

Technique

# Parent Storytelling

## When to Use the Technique

Anxiety reactions, some depressive states, and acting out in response to repressed emotions are usefully addressed through this technique.

## Patient Age and Profile

Preschool children may prefer to hear of a baby elephant, while school-age children may do better with tales of a lion or bear cub. Young children are often enthralled with stories of any kind and may not be aware they are receiving a therapeutic message. School-age children may "get it," that they are being subtly instructed, but enjoy the process of being told a story so that they are willing to hear it, even repeatedly, which serves to underline the message.

## How the Technique Works

Exposure to anxiety-provoking situations has been shown to be useful in reducing fears and anxieties. The purpose of having the parents tell these stories is to reassure the child that hidden feelings are acceptable and that opening up about them will make the child feel better. It is important, therefore, that these stories embody the feelings that the child feels reluctant to reveal.

In the parents' telling of the stories, the animal characters feel better by acknowledging these same feelings to other characters in the story. This message is reassuring to the child. Parents may now be giving the child a very different, and hopefully more beneficial, kind of attention than he or she had previously been receiving. A final benefit to the parents is that by giving them something to help their children, they can change their own feelings of helplessness and frustration.

## Indicators/Measures of Success

Parents often feel insecure about their ability to tell coherent, creative stories. It may be necessary for the therapist to provide some skeletal stories that embody the child's repressed feelings. Parents need to be reassured that their creativity is not an issue here. What is important is that they are communicating an important lesson about self-acceptance to their children in a fun, non-threatening way that also brings parent

---

### Definition

In parent storytelling, the therapist instructs the parent to first identify what a child is grappling with emotionally and then tell a story that incorporates the child's feelings or fears. The story uses imaginary characters (young animals such as tiger cubs or baby elephants) that express the same type of feeling the child is having difficulty with. This is usually more effective than using real-life stories, which include situations in the parent's life or day-to-day interactions. In the stories, the character feels relief by telling someone about the feelings that are troubling him or her and is shown that others have the same problems.

and child closer together. Parents need to be willing to continue to do these story sessions on their own at home, on an ongoing basis. Children who are troubled about unacceptable feelings and impulses will receive palpable relief from this intervention on a dynamic as well as family level.

## Suggested Readings and Resources

Wachtel, E. *Treating Troubled Children and Their Families*. New York: Guilford Press, 1994.

Brett, D. *Annie Stories*. New York: Workman, 1986.

Mills, J. & Crowley, R. *Therapeutic Metaphors for Children and the Child Within*. New York: Brunner/Mazel, 1986.

# Pattern Interruption

The most important aspect of pattern intervention is discovering the sequence of behaviors that most typically surround the problem behavior and then altering or adding to it. For example, a student who blurts out answers elicits reprimands or ignoring of the behavior by the teacher. If this doesn't work, the teacher might interrupt the pattern by asking the child to move to a "blurting" desk. If a boy habitually sucks his thumb, and it is always the right thumb, then the left thumb "needs equal time"—thus altering the habit. A mother who habitually "nags" is asked to write her "nags" on paper and hand them to her child.

### Definition

Pattern interruption is based on the notion that all behaviors, including negative ones, may become automatic reactions to stressful situations. Pattern interruption attempts to alter a small part of the reaction pattern, thereby making the behavior more conscious and the person thus more able to control it.

## When to Use the Technique

Almost any kind of habitual chain of actions and reactions would lend itself to this type of intervention. Bad habits, circular arguments, unfruitful discussions or punishments, and consequences that have no effect on behavior would be the kinds of problems where pattern interruption should be considered.

## Patient Age and Profile

For older children who want to change something in their own behavior, this technique could provide a shortcut. With younger children, it would probably be more efficient to work on the parents' reactions if they are willing. In either case, this is a technique that requires a fairly high level of rapport and compliance for the client(s) to be willing to try something different.

## How the Technique Works

Suggestions offered in this approach must make sense to the "customer"; thus a reframe is often necessary before suggesting a pattern interruption. The reframe is a new way of thinking, and this technique offers a new way of doing. For change to happen, both seem necessary.

## Indicators/Measures of Success

Because you are trying to change a very small aspect of behavior, it is rather easy to assess whether this change has occurred. If the small change does occur, there may be large benefits. The client has enjoyed a success experience at changing something. Rather than looking for generalization of this change, as might be construed in behavior therapy, practitioners look for a small change to set in motion the possibilities of greater change. Any control, no matter how small, that is restored to the individual or family in a previously out-of-control situation presents hope and a sense of power that is useful for tackling greater changes.

## Suggested Readings and Resources

O'Hanlon, W. *Taproots: Underlying Principles of Milton H. Erickson's Therapy and Hypnosis.* New York: W. W. Norton, 1987.

Molnar, A., and B. Lindquist. *Changing Problem Behavior in Schools.* San Francisco: Jossey-Bass, 1989.

# Peer Mediation

### When to Use the Technique

Children who are prone to anger or aggression will obviously have more conflict than the average child, and so it is that much more important that they learn to resolve disputes in a constructive manner.

### Patient Age and Profile

Children of all ages can benefit from this technique, but adolescents may find it to be most effective.

### How the Technique Works

Typically, children with problems in anger control will have constant verbal and physical fights. Although it is desirable that children always demonstrate "good behavior," this is not realistic. Conflict is a normal part of life, and children must learn how to resolve it in a constructive way. Mediation allows children to work out their differences in a nonjudgmental environment. The goal is not to determine guilt or innocence but rather to work out differences constructively. Mediation provides a way to address problems that allows children in conflict to discuss their grievances in a neutral, confidential setting. Anger issues and the antisocial behavior resulting from them are the most common problems dealt with in mediation.

Mediation activities create a friendly environment, enhance listening skills, teach participants to respond to a conflict from both points of view, teach participants to analyze verbal and nonverbal responses, identify reasons why people argue or fight, identify common methods used to handle conflict, identify common emotions that people have in a conflict, distinguish between a feeling and desired action, and identify the clues that act as signals of conflict.

The elements of peer mediation include:

- listening carefully
- being fair
- asking how each person feels

## ᵒ Definition

Peer mediation is defined as "a process of resolving disputes and conflicts with peers with the help of a neutral third party, a mediator, who facilitates the process." Mediation is an effective way for the angry child to try to resolve conflicts, because the problem is externalized and the child's self-esteem is not threatened.

- letting each person state what happened

- treating each person with respect

- keeping what you are told confidential

- mediating in private

- not taking sides

- not telling the parties what to do

- not asking who started it

- not blaming anyone for the situation

- not asking, "Why did you do it?"

- not giving advice

- not looking for witnesses.

## Indicators/Measures of Success

If the conflict is resolved after following the above steps, the peer mediation can be considered successful.

## Forms

The Mediation Cards (pages 205-206) can be used to help teach children the mediation process. In teaching children how to be peer mediators, the adult should act as a "coach" to the child mediator. The Mediation Cards can be used as "cue cards" to help the child mediator move the mediation along in the appropriate direction.

## Suggested Readings and Resources

Schmidt, F., and A. Friedman. *Fighting Fair: Dr. Martin Luther King for Kids.* Miami Beach: Peace Education Foundation, 1990.

Schmidt, F., A. Friedman, and J. Marvel. *Mediation for Kids.* Miami Beach: Peace Education Foundation, 1992.

Sorenson, D. *Conflict Resolution and Mediation for Peer Helpers.* Minneapolis: Educational Media Corp., 1992.

# Playing Baby

## When to Use the Technique

Children who involve their parents in provocative and negative ways are often acting out difficult-to-acknowledge dependency needs. If the negative behaviors elicit highly involved parental responses, they may develop a momentum of their own. This technique can be useful for either these acting-out "tough" children or children more obviously in need of dependent nurturing (anxious or immature children).

## Patient Age and Profile

Because the directions can be adapted to the comfort level of the children and parents, this approach can be modified until early adolescence. It is especially relevant for preschool children, children whose inappropriate actions demand a great deal of attention, and school-age children who need a "regressive vacation."

## How the Technique Works

All growing up is "two steps forward and one step back." If the step back is resisted by either parent or child, then immature or acting-out behaviors may increase in intensity. This approach attempts to make a playful ritual out of otherwise troubling demands for attention and nurturing. By having the parents initiate playing baby when the child is already behaving well, the need for acting out to raise the intensity of the parent-child connection is short circuited. By having the parent initiate, the child does not need to ask for what he or she may not know is wanted—a return to a less challenging time of childhood.

Playing baby games and making statements ("No matter how big you are, there is part of you that will always be my baby") not only symbolically addresses the child's needs but also may change the nature of the parent-child interaction. Child provocations and parental pamperings are brought under more conscious control through these activities.

### Definition

In playing baby, parents are asked to initiate activities that communicate to the child the notion that even though he or she is expected to act in an age-appropriate manner, in some sense the child will always be the parent's "baby." These activities will vary greatly depending on the personality and age of the child and how comfortable the parents are with this type of play. Some parents may have a lot of fun bringing back the school-age child's "blankie" or pretending the child is an infant. For others, toddler-type first steps or crawling might be more fun. Some families may simply reminisce about the joys of babyhood and view old family photos together.

## Indicators/Measures of Success

This technique may work on several levels: the child's awareness, the parent's understanding of the underlying message of a child's behavior, and parent-child interaction. Resistance to this technique, which should never be forced on an unwilling parent, can give important clues as to the direction future sessions need to take.

## Suggested Readings and Resources

Oaklander, V. *Helping Children and Adolescents Become Self-Nurturing*. Seattle: Max Sound Tape Co., 1986.

_____. *Windows to Our Children*. Highland, NY: Center for Gestalt Development, 1988.

Wachtel, E. *Treating Troubled Children and Their Families*. New York: Guilford Press, 1994.

# Prediction Task

## When to Use the Technique

Problems that seem to occur randomly but are potentially under the patient's control are best served by this technique.

## Patient Age and Profile

Children ages 6 and up are right for this technique.

## How the Technique Works

Paradoxical techniques of this nature change the patient's perception of the problem and usually work because of some underlying behavioral principle. In the case cited above, the enuretic child was motivated to make a behavioral intervention and was reinforced by his success.

In an example cited by Selekman (1997), Rico, a 9-year-old boy, was brought in for therapy by his mother, Marcella, for bad temper tantrums that occurred on the average "four times per week." Marcella was unaware of what she or Rico was doing on the other three days of the week that made them "good" days. The twosome typically fought over doing schoolwork, watching too much TV, and buying toys Rico wanted. Rico was very athletic and was a Michael Jordan fan.

Selekman gave Marcella and Rico the following prediction task. Separately, the night before the next day, Rico and Marcella were to predict whether the next day would be a "good" day (no tantrums) and to try to account for what made it a good day. One week later the family reported a number of changes, including fewer power struggles and only one tantrum. Marcella was so pleased she bought Rico the Michael Jordan T-shirt he wanted.

## Indicators/Measures of Success

Since this technique is used mostly for discrete behaviors, it can be measured by a behavioral recording chart (see below). A baseline of the behavior should be taken before the intervention.

### Definition

This technique is a type of paradoxical intention, where a child is asked to predict when something that seems out of control will occur. For example, a boy who is a random bedwetter is asked to predict whether he will wet the bed that night. When he says "no," he begins to understand that he has the ability to control his problem if he chooses or to get the help necessary to control the problem. In one instance, an 8-year-old child predicted that he would not wet his bed for a week and set his alarm clock for 3 a.m. each night so that he could urinate. Before the prediction task, his parents described him as being uncooperative and unmotivated in addressing his enuresis. After the prediction task was effective, he was described as "in control and aware of his problem."

## Suggested Readings and Resources

de Shazer, S. *Keys to Solutions in Brief Therapy.* New York: W. W. Norton, 1985.

Technique

# Prescribing the Symptom

## When to Use the Technique

This technique is used primarily with families that have become stuck in rigid behavior patterns, ones that have proved highly resistant to change by more direct methods.

## Patient Age and Profile

Family members of all ages can benefit from this technique.

## How the Technique Works

This technique is related to paradoxical intentionality, a technique devised by Viktor Frankl who used it to treat obsessive or anxious patients. By asking the clients to exaggerate a symptom that had been out of their control, Frankl gave control back to the client by having him or her "do it more." This approach is likened to "steering into a skid" on a wet or icy road; a gentle going with the deviation is more likely to get the car, or client, back on the road.

In this ploy the therapist, who is being consulted to help people change, is telling them not to change. Such an assignment is considered to lower resistance to change by rendering it unnecessary. Meanwhile, the therapist has given the family or client a possible explanation for why the symptom is occurring (family harmony or homeostasis). The therapist thus challenges the function or purpose of the symptom. The unstated rules by which the participants operated becomes more obvious to them, as does the idea that their previous behavior "just happened" involuntarily but can't be brought under voluntary control.

This confrontation with the individual's or family's underlying rules is designed to "unbalance" the system and force the clients to engage in new and more appropriate behavior. It is the confrontational style that makes this approach difficult for many therapists, who may see it as manipulative or unnecessarily harsh.

## Indicators/Measures of Success

This approach is cleverly constructed to create a win/win situation for the therapist. If the family listens and does what you say, then you have

### Definition

Prescribing the symptom is a form of the therapeutic double bind. In this technique a client (or family) is instructed to continue or even to exaggerate what he or she is already doing. For example, if two siblings are fighting regularly, they are asked to continue to do so, possibly even more frequently. If the client (or family) obeys the therapist, then he or she has ceded control and let the therapist in, to give advice and coach. If the client (or family) resists the therapist's injunction, even better, for then he or she is no longer behaving in a symptomatic way.

THE THERAPIST'S TOOLBOX

new leverage and power in the family. If the family members do not listen, or if they oppose the prescription to do more of the symptom, then they are changing their patterns of behavior.

## Suggested Readings and Resources

Haley, J. *Problem-solving Therapy*. San Francisco: Jossey-Bass, 1976.

Weeks, G., and L. L'Abate. *Paradoxical Psychotherapy: Theory and Technique*. New York: Brunner/Mazel, 1982.

Technique

# Pretending to Have the Symptom

## When to Use the Technique

Interactive behavior patterns within families often take on a life of their own. Nobody intends for dysfunctional behavior to become ingrained in the life of a family, but sometimes actions and reactions flow in a cyclical manner that reinforces the negative aspects of each side's attempts at resolution (i.e., the more the child has temper tantrums, the more the parent reacts with anger and frustration, then withdrawal, which leads to more temper tantrums, etc.). These negative spirals have been treated with reported success by paradoxical techniques. Pretending to have the symptom is playful and doesn't arouse family resistance or depend on noncompliance the way prescribing the symptom would.

## Patient Age and Profile

This technique can be used with any family or individual who is willing to comply and actively tries to employ it. Like most paradoxical techniques, it works best on repetitive, mindless behavior patterns that have been resistant to more direct approaches.

## How the Technique Works

If one "pretends" to behave in a way that one has been behaving, it follows that (a) he or she is more in control of the behavior, (b) what had been viewed as destructive may become fun and relaxed, (c) if other family members pretend to react the way they have been reacting to the original behavior, then everyone enjoys more of a gamelike atmosphere, and (d) all become more flexible and begin to vary their behaviors, bringing on even more flexibility.

The steps of this intervention are as follows: (1) the therapist forms a picture of the symptomatic behavior pattern—who does what, followed by what reaction, followed by what reaction, etc.; (2) the therapist assesses if the family will likely cooperate with requests; (3) the therapist asks the participants to pretend to enact the problem in the session. The initiator is told to pretend to do what is usually done, followed by the others' pretend reactions in their characteristic ways; (4) the therapist asks for the scene to be reenacted, but this time the therapist prescribes

### Definition

This technique is a paradoxical intervention designed to be a gentler way of effecting change in the family than prescribing the symptom. In the "pretending to have the symptom" approach, the therapist carefully instructs the family members to pretend, and continue to pretend, to do what they have been already doing, albeit formerly not within their control (i.e., you can't pretend to have temper tantrums and really have temper tantrums at the same time). To use this approach successfully, the therapist must adequately understand the meaning and purpose of the symptomatic behavior and intervene accordingly.

additional behavior that changes it or highlights its meaning; (5) the therapist prescribes the sequence as homework to be repeated several times before the next session; and (6) at the next session the family reports what has happened.

## Indicators/Measures of Success

If significant behavior change occurs in the individual or family practicing this pretense, then the therapist may accept real change as an outcome or request that the family continue the pretend task as a way of reinforcing the change. The success depends to a large extent on the therapist understanding the meaning of the symptom in a way that takes into account the context.

## Suggested Readings and Resources

Madanes, C. *Strategic Family Therapy.* San Francisco: Jossey Bass, 1981.

Nichols, M. *Family Therapy: Concepts and Methods.* New York: Gardner Press, 1984.

# Preventive Intervention

### When to Use the Technique

ADHD children who have trouble controlling their actions and behavior can benefit from this intervention.

### Patient Age and Profile

Young children with impulsivity problems are the most promising group for this therapy.

### How the Technique Works

Methods of reducing incidents of misbehavior within the preventive intervention paradigm include: (1) anticipating possible misbehaviors and teaching the child skills for good behavior, and (2) anticipating possible misbehaviors and controlling the environment in such a way that specific misbehaviors are impossible to commit.

This technique is illustrated by the following example:

Joey is an 8-year-old ADHD boy who enjoys watching TV. His mother frequently scolds him for not washing his hands before he goes into the family room. Today, after Joey eats his French fries and heads for the couch, his mother intercepts him and explains that she doesn't like grease on the remote control (or other objects) and that touching objects after touching greasy foods will make them greasy. She checks for understanding by making Joey repeat her instructions and tapes a note to the remote control that states, "Wash hands before touching." She then returns to the kitchen but casually observes Joey's behavior.

The principles involved in this process include:

- *Anticipating the misbehavior.* In this example, the mother anticipates that Joey will soil something with his greasy hands.

- *Preventing the misbehavior by educating the child.* The mother makes Joey aware that touching objects with greasy hands will soil them, and that this is unacceptable. She uses positive direction in a short, specific manner.

## Definition

Preventive intervention is a method of behavioral management that focuses on preventing misbehavior before it happens. It involves anticipating a misbehavior and educating a child as to how to behave properly in a given situation before the misbehavior actually takes place. This can be accomplished through either education or controlling the environment.

Often, positive reinforcement is beneficial when used in conjunction with preventive education. ADHD children need immediate reinforcement as incentives to better behavior. In the previous example, the mother can reward Joey by allowing him to have a later bedtime if he washes his hands before touching other objects. She can say, "You've been very good at not touching the remote control without washing your hands. You can stay up half an hour later tonight to watch more TV."

Preventive intervention can also involve controlling the environment so that specific misbehaviors are impossible. For example:

Betty is a 6 year old with ADHD who likes to play with her mother's make-up. Sometimes her mother thinks this is cute, but lately she is becoming annoyed by the mess. Finally, the mother locks her make-up in a drawer to prevent the problem altogether. She has anticipated and identified the problem behavior, identified the principal objects in the problem behavior, and altered the environment so that the principal objects are shielded from the child.

The appropriateness of a specific preventive intervention depends on the age of the child. Anticipating misbehavior and controlling the environment of a toddler is far easier than controlling the environment of an 8 year old. Education is a more appropriate strategy for older children. For behaviors that pose a serious threat to the child or others, preventive controlling of the environment is the safer method, with preventive education used as a supplement.

## Indicators/Measures of Success

When the environment has been controlled and the anticipated outcome has been achieved, this technique can be considered successful.

## Suggested Readings and Resources

Goldstein, S., and M. Goldstein. *Hyperactivity: Why Won't My Child Pay Attention?* New York: Wiley, 1992.

_____. *Managing Attention Disorders in Children: A Guide for Practitioners.* New York: Wiley, 1990.

Technique

# Problem-Solving Therapy

In problem-solving therapy, the therapist works first and foremost with the presenting symptom. While doing so, the therapist keeps in mind that the problem lies within the whole social unit—the family, school, or community. Rather than try to convince the family that it is the whole system that is malfunctioning, interventions are designed so that all are involved in the child's environment.

Haley, in his 1988 book, offers the following guidelines in working with a family who bring a problematic child in for therapy: The therapist can focus on (1) the child; (2) the parent-child unit; or (3) the parent-child-parent triangle. Usually one parent is intensely involved with the child while the other one is more peripheral. Knowing this, the therapist can choose a way to intervene:

*Approach 1*: *Entering through the peripheral person.* This is the most traditional approach in family therapy. The disengaged parent may have become that way due to criticism from the overinvolved parent and thus may be reluctant to get involved. When the overinvolved parent is excluded from primary interaction with the child, the parents begin to draw together into a more cohesive unit. It is important that the therapist not imply that the engaged parent has failed, thus necessitating the involvement of the disengaged parent. The need for the disengaged parent to get involved can be explained as important for the child's development.

*Approach 2*: *Entering through the more involved parent.* In this case, the peripheral person is put in an advisory or supportive role. The involved parent is not told to disengage from the child, nor is the overinvolvement explicitly discussed. Instead, the overinvolved parent is simply guided into more appropriate interactions with the child. It is important that the overinvolved parent begin to develop his or her own interests that are independent of the child.

*Approach 3*: *Entering through the parents conjointly.* This is usually the best approach if the child is showing severe problems. Although it may not appear so at first, in cases of violent, psychotic, suicidal, or substance-abusing behavior from the child, both parents are generally equally involved. It is important that the parents both be clear about their plans

## Definition

Problem-solving therapy focuses on solving an individual's problems by looking at the family and social context. The therapist examines the presenting problem and then implements an intervention. Problem-solving therapy was developed by Jay Haley, whose work was influenced by Gregory Bateson, Milton Erickson, Salvador Minuchin, Braulio Montalvo, and Cloe Madanes. Like other family therapies, this approach revolves around the belief that symptoms can be viewed as appropriate and adaptive behavior and thus the focus is on the social context rather than the symptom in isolation.

for the child. If the child has been away from the home due to outside intervention, it is especially critical that the parents present a united front when the child returns home.

## When to Use the Technique

This type of therapy has been used with a variety of disorders, including childhood depression, conduct disorders, and eating disorders, especially where it is assessed that the child's symptoms are due to dysfunctional patterns in the family. It would not be appropriate for disorders that have strong hereditary components.

## Patient Age and Profile

The age of the child is not a factor in the use of this treatment.

## How the Technique Works

This school of therapy assumes that a symptom does not exist in isolation, but rather is an adaptive response to one's environment and needs to be treated accordingly.

## Indicators/Measures of Success

This technique targets on a specific problem or symptom and should result in a measurable decrease in the presenting problem within 12 to 16 sessions.

## Suggested Readings and Resources

Haley, J. *Problem Solving Therapy.* San Francisco: Jossey Bass, 1987.

Technique

# Rational Emotive Therapy

RET was one of the first forms of cognitive behavioral therapy. In 1955, New York psychologist Albert Ellis founded the technique in response to his frustration with what he considered to be the inefficient and unsatisfactory results of psychoanalysis.

RET is based upon what Ellis calls the "ABC framework." "A" stands for an activating event. The event may be either internal or external and is influential to the person. "B" stands for beliefs. These are the evaluative types of thoughts the person has, beliefs that may be either rational or irrational. Irrational beliefs tend to be very rigid and can take on several different forms: (a) awfulizing, in which a conclusion that is reached about something is far worse than it needs to be; (b) low frustration tolerance (lft), in which the person can absolutely not even stand the thought of something; or (c) damnation, in which the person "damns" himself or herself, other people, and life in general. Flexible beliefs are considered to be rational and are more adaptive. The conclusions drawn from these beliefs are based upon rational premises. These conclusions can take several forms: (a) evaluation of "badness," in which the person evaluates how bad a situation is, realizing that it could be worse; (b) statements of toleration, in which the person acknowledges that he or she does not like something but is able to live with it; or (c) acceptance of fallibility, in which the person accepts personal and world conditions, also recognizing that people are fallible.

"C" stands for consequences, both emotional and behavioral, that result from the person's beliefs about "A." The consequences that result from irrational and rigid beliefs are considered inappropriate, and consequences that result from rational and flexible beliefs are termed appropriate. To put the framework together, there are activating events ("A") that spark off evaluative beliefs ("B") that lead to the feelings and behaviors in "C." The three components work together, interacting and influencing each other (Dryden, 1990).

In order for a client to change, three major insights must be internalized:

***Insight #1:*** Past or present events do not cause negative emotional or behavioral consequences. Rather, it is a person's belief system about the activating events that leads to negative feelings and behaviors.

## Definition

Rational emotive therapy (RET) emphasizes the difference between an actual event and a person's interpretation of the event. Clients are helped to change the negative way that they interpret events and learn more positive ways to interpret and evaluate situations.

*Insight #2:* Regardless of how the person has felt in the past, it is due to current irrational beliefs that he or she is not happy.

*Insight #3:* People find it easy to cling to self-defeating thoughts, feelings, and actions. This can be overcome by continually working to dispute irrational beliefs and the effects they have.

Linscott and DiGiuseppe (1994) recommend that RET with children be done over the course of 17 sessions that last from 45 to 60 minutes each. In a school setting, if the parents are not available, the child's teacher can be included in the treatment plan. The authors present the following guidelines for the 17-session course of therapy:

*Session 1.* The therapist meets with the child and the parents. The parents are given the chance to describe the problem from their perspective(s), and then the child is given the chance to give his or her perspective. The therapist presents an understanding of the situation and treatment goals and plans are discussed. The task of therapy is discussed, and any standardized tests that might be helpful are administered.

*Session 2.* The therapist meets with the parents alone. The parents' role in the child's problem is assessed, and a working alliance is developed between the therapist and the parents.

*Session 3.* The therapist works with the child to increase his or her vocabulary of emotions and to discuss the intensity of emotions. The idea of a "feeling thermometer" is introduced, with 1 on the thermometer representing no feeling and 10 representing very intense feeling. The child learns the difference between helpful and hurtful emotions and a goal is set of feeling helpful emotions rather than hurtful ones in distressing situations.

*Session 4.* The child learns that it is thoughts that cause emotions rather than events. The therapist introduces the idea that incorrect thoughts lead to hurtful emotions, and correct thoughts lead to helpful emotions. The child is also given a rationale for learning to produce helpful feelings rather than hurtful ones.

*Session 5.* The child learns how to identify rational thoughts versus irrational thoughts. The therapist has the child practice substituting helpful thoughts for hurtful ones. Rational, helpful thoughts are connected to positive emotional and behavioral consequences.

*Session 6.* In this session, the child learns how to challenge his or her thoughts and look for those thoughts that are disturbing or hurtful. The child is also taught to change harmful thoughts to more helpful ones.

**Session 7.** The child learns about the concept of self-rating. The therapist discusses the fact that everyone has strengths and weaknesses and that both are acceptable. The child learns that weaknesses can be improved and made into strengths.

**Session 8.** The child and the therapist talk about expressing feelings. The benefit of discussing emotions versus not discussing them is debated and appropriate times to do both is covered. The child learns appropriate places, times, and ways to communicate emotions.

**Session 9.** The therapist teaches the child that everyone makes mistakes and that this does not make someone a bad person. The fact that worrying about making a mistake can lead to making that mistake is talked about, and the concept that people can learn from their mistakes is discussed. The child learns coping statements that can be used after a mistake has been made.

**Session 10.** The idea that it is good to ask for help when necessary is introduced. The consequences of not asking for help are explored, and the child learns the behavioral skills involved in asking for help.

**Session 11.** The goal of this session is to increase the child's tolerance for frustration. The child learns to rate how difficult a task is and differentiate which ones are too hard to attempt.

**Session 12.** The child learns ways to cope with the criticism of peers. The child learns that self-esteem does not have to based entirely upon others' opinions.

**Sessions 13 through 16.** These sessions are used for review and closure. Specific incidents may be brought in either by the child or the parents for discussion in the sessions. The therapist assesses which skills need further work at this point and focuses attention on these areas.

**Session 17.** Final closure is obtained in this session. The course of therapy is reviewed, and the child is helped to acknowledge all the new skills gained. The family is praised for its accomplishments, and areas for future work are described. Termination generally occurs during this session; however, if it is indicated, additional sessions can be contracted for at this point.

## When to Use the Technique

Because this is a highly intellectual format, RET is recommended for older children and adolescents who are verbal and at least somewhat motivated to change. It has been used with clients who have interpersonal problems, various anxieties, and with high-risk adolescents.

## Patient Age and Profile

RET was originally designed to be used with adults. The outline for children presented here was designed by Linscott and DiGiuseppe and is for ages 8 through 12.

## How the Technique Works

Ellis' formulation of RET in many ways parallels the development of cognitive behavioral therapy as practiced by Beck and his associates. Although the terminology and techniques differ, both share the assumption that there is a link between thoughts, feelings, and behaviors, and when you change one (usually thoughts), the others will change as well.

## Indicators/Measures of Success

Since RET is considered a total treatment program its efficacy can be measured by pre- and post-treatment tests specific to the referring problem.

## Suggested Readings and Resources

Ellis, A., and M. Bernard, eds. *Rational Emotive Approaches to the Problems of Childhood.* New York: Plenum Press, 1983.

Dryden, W. *Dealing With Anger Problems: Rational-Emotive Therapeutic Interventions.* Sarasota, FL: Professional Resource Exchange, 1990.

Linscott, J., and R. DiGiuseppe. "Rational Emotive Therapy with Children." *Handbook of Child and Adolescent Treatment Manuals.* New York: Lexington Books, 1994.

Technique

# Reframing

Reframing can often be helpful as an antidote to children given a negative, pathological label. A child who is considered disruptive or uncooperative may be reframed as awkward or lacking self-confidence; a lazy child may be relabeled as "laid back." Conversely, teacher and parents can be usefully relabeled as well; for example, the demanding, critical teacher can be relabeled as having high standards for his or her students.

## When to Use the Technique

Reframing is potentially effective in situations that have become "stuck," where there are rigid, inflexible views of reality. This rigidity contributes to the maintenance of the problem behavior.

The therapist must seek a reasonable fit between the reframe and the problem, but proponents of this technique have pointed out that any situation involves multiple truths, and that initial skepticism by clients may change after they have had time to think about the reframe.

## Patient Age and Profile

This intervention is effective with families and with problems of a relationship nature. Virtually all ages of children can benefit from reframing as part of their treatment.

## How the Technique Works

Many therapists consider reframing to be the most basic and essential intervention to effect change. When people come to therapy, by definition, their ways of viewing the problem have become nonproductive. There needs to be a change in their perception of the problem that will enable them to react to it differently. Reframing began with therapists' noticing how families label symptomatic behavior and how changing that label can influence the interactions of families.

Another form of reframing is "positive connotation," wherein the symptomatic behavior is seen as positive because it helps the family as a whole. By suggesting a good motive for troubling behavior ("The reason your child won't go to school is because he wants to keep his lonely

### Definition

Reframing is the verbal relabeling of behavior by putting it into a new, usually more positive, perspective. Reframing offers change by opening up the possibility of different responses and seeing a problem in a different way. It was devised by family systems therapists for use with "stuck" families but has been extended to use with individuals in a variety of settings.

mother company"), the family begins to look at the behavior as an attempt to maintain harmony. If the child's behavior is seen not as "sick" but as intentional (though misguided), then the family can more readily accept that the behavior may be negative but that the goal is positive. The intervention makes it easier for the family to accept the child and for the child to view his or her own behavior as controllable.

Reframing, long before it was called this, was a precondition for any change. Good teachers, healers, and other change agents have recognized the need to change what we call the problem, or at least what we consider aspects of that problem.

## Indicators/Measures of Success

Reframing is considered successful if the rigid definition of an individual's behavior begins to be seen as more complex. If that change can lead to a wider range of responses—for the individual, for the family, or for the teachers—then the technique has succeeded. If power struggles or any nonproductive attempts to influence others' behavior can stop due to reframing, then it has "done its job."

## Suggested Readings and Resources

Andolfi, M. *Family Therapy: An Interactional Approach*. New York: Plenum, 1979.

Cade, B., and W. O'Hanlon. *A Brief Guide to Brief Therapy*. New York: W. W. Norton, 1993.

Durrant, M. *Creative Strategies for School Problems: Solutions for Psychologists and Teachers*. New York: W. W. Norton. 1995.

Technique

# Response Prevention

### Definition

Response prevention is a behavioral technique that attempts to break the connection between a specific stimulus and a dysfunctional behavior. For example, suppose that a child with an obsessive-compulsive disorder feels the need to wash his or her hands immediately after touching a door knob. The child would be gradually exposed to the situation that is upsetting (i.e., seeing the door knob, getting closer to the door knob, lightly touching it, then gripping and turning it) while the hand-washing would be prevented. Response prevention is used with systematic exposure to the object that causes fear or anxiety.

## When to Use the Technique

Response prevention is most frequently used for obsessive-compulsive disorders and specific phobias.

## Patient Age and Profile

This behavioral technique is generally not used until children are 4 or 5 but theoretically could be used with a client of any age.

## How the Technique Works

The assumption here is that lack of adequate exposure to the feared object maintains the level of anxiety associated with it. Systematic exposure to the feared object breaks the link of conditioned ritual or avoidance responses.

## Indicators/Measures of Success

Success is measured by tracking a decline in the targeted dysfunctional behavior.

## Suggested Readings and Resources

March, J. "Cognitive-Behavioral Psychotherapy for Children and Adolescents with OCD: A Review and Recommendations for Treatment." *Journal of the American Academy of Child and Adolescent Psychiatry,* 34(1), 7-18, 1995.

# Reworking

## When to Use the Technique

This technique seems to be particularly helpful for children who have been abused or otherwise traumatized, giving them a sense of power over past events.

## Patient Age and Profile

The technique works best with children over age 7, who have developed a sense of the progression of time.

## How the Technique Works

Based on psychodynamic as well as humanistic theories of psychology, the validity of this technique is supported by current research on the way that the emotional brain develops. The therapeutic power of this technique is derived from the sense of mastery and completion the child experiences and the cognitive understanding that one can gain control over distressful emotional states.

## Indicators/Measures of Success

When the child is reworking the artwork as a therapeutic exercise, the intervention is successful.

## Suggested Readings and Resources

Gil, E. *The Healing Power of Play.* New York: Guilford Press, 1991.

### Definition

Reworking is an art therapy concept that encourages children to keep a chronological portfolio of their artwork, preferably in a pad or in a book, so that they can go back and make changes to earlier drawings. Having the opportunity to go back and make corrections or changes gives children a sense of mastery and is a metaphor for their being able to change past hurts or problematic behaviors.

Technique

# Role Reversal

## When to Use the Technique

This technique is helpful with any kind of habitual, reciprocal relationship issue that has evolved into rigid roles: nagger-sulker, leader-follower, overcompetent-incompetent, pursuer-avoider, etc. When people are insensitive to each other's effect on the other, or are at an impasse over a particular issue, role reversal can be a useful intervention. This technique is especially useful in situations where greater empathy and appreciation of another's position might be important to unblock stalemates.

## Patient Age and Profile

Adolescents or preadolescent children who have become mired in repetitive conflicts with their parents or siblings are the ideal population for role reversal. It is doubly beneficial to have them role play their parent or sibling and for them to witness their parent or sibling's role playing of them. Any family members who need help resolving a particular issue and are capable of taking over someone else's role can participate, but very young preschool children find it difficult to leave behind their own egotistical view of the world.

## How the Technique Works

Role reversal was originally devised by Moreno and his psychodrama associates. It has been adapted by family therapists for use with couples and families and by conflict-resolution experts in school settings.

While the technique is being played out, the therapist encourages the dialog, observes verbal and nonverbal communication, reflects, questions, asks for clarification, and interprets. Other players may be involved as assistants or alter egos. Questions such as "Why do you think that person is doing that?" "What do you want to do now?" "What could you do differently?" and "How does it feel right now?" extend the learning potential of this technique.

The assumption is that the issue or relationship will look and feel different if the members exchange places. Problems occur when roles

### Definition

In role reversal, a person is asked to exchange places with another person with whom they may be in conflict. It is a technique that assesses the ability to see the situation through the eyes of the other and allows one to emotionally experience the other's viewpoint. Role reversal yields data as to how well family members (or teachers and students) know each other and pay attention to each other's feelings and offers an opportunity to experiment with other ways of seeing or experiencing the world.

become locked into dysfunctional patterns; participants in these patterns are likely to try to resolve these "locks" by doing more of the same (i.e., the parent yells louder at the disobedient child). The purpose of role reversal is to: (1) break a usual pattern; (2) try new behaviors that are part of a new role; (3) work on an area that each needs to enhance; (4) reduce conflict; and (5) "walk a mile" in the other's shoes. In complementary roles, where each is necessary to form a whole, this technique allows the participants to stop focusing on the parts each one plays and begin to see the whole—their interdependence.

## Indicators/Measures of Success

Seeing the world from the other person's point of view is the primary goal. The change in behavior—the breaking of the pattern—is the ultimate indication of success. After the technique, participants are questioned as to what they felt and how they would like things to change. These changes are then incorporated as homework assignments in order to effect the greatest change.

## Suggested Readings and Resources

Minuchin, S., and H. Fishman. *Family Therapy Techniques.* Cambridge, MA: Harvard University Press, 1981.

Moreno, J. *Psychodrama.* New York: Beacon House, 1946.

_____. *Sociometry, Experimental Method and the Science of Society.* New York: Beacon House, 1951.

# The Rosebush Technique

## Example

Oaklander asked children to imagine that they were rosebushes and then asked a series of specific questions such as the following: Do you have flowers? What color are they? Do you have leaves? What do they look like? Do you have thorns? Roots? Where are you planted? Are there other rosebushes around or are you alone?

Dr. Oaklander then asked the children to draw pictures of the rosebush, and finally she talked to the children in the present tense ("Are you a happy rosebush?" "Who takes care of you?") The session concluded by asking the children if there were anything they said as rosebushes that reminded them of themselves and their own situation.

## When to Use the Technique

This type of technique is helpful to children and adolescents with internalized disorders, such as anxiety reactions, fears, depression, PTSD, and so on.

## Patient Age and Profile

This technique could be used with children ages 5 and up. Since it is primarily a verbal technique, naturally it would be recommended for children who are verbally expressive. Older children may gain insight from interpretation of their responses.

## How the Technique Works

Projective techniques are useful for making cognitive connections to unarticulated emotions or emotional memories.

## Indicators/Measures of Success

Recording responses and referring back to the child's pictures can be a useful way to chart progress in a child's therapy. This is an example of a technique where a diagnostic technique can also be used for treatment purposes.

### Definition

Projective imagery can be useful to ascertain a child's self-image. Violet Oaklander (1988) suggested using the metaphor of a rosebush to help children reveal a sense of their overall image, their vulnerability, defense mechanisms, and so on.

## Suggested Readings and Resources

Oaklander, V. *Windows in Our Children: A Gestalt Therapy Approach to Children and Adolescents.*
Highland, NY: Gestalt Journal Press, 1988.

Technique

# Sandplay/Sand Tray Therapy

In Sandplay therapy, the child is given a small box that has a width and length generally not bigger than 23 x 28 inches with a 2 or 3 inch lip. The box is filled with sand, and the child is given his or her choice of figures of all types, which might include people, cars, trees, animals, fences, buildings, rocks, bushes, airplanes, guns, cannons, birds, windmills, and ships. The child is asked to create a scene of any type using any or all the figures. The picture that the child creates is considered to be a three-dimensional representation of some aspect of the child's psychic situation. Just as a drama can be acted out, the picture is thought to be transposed from the inner world to the outer world (Kalff, 1980).

## When to Use the Technique

In the United States, this technique seems to be most frequently used with children who have experienced a trauma. It allows the child to slowly deal with memories and anxieties in a symbolic context.

## Patient Age and Profile

The technique is generally used with children over the age of 5.

## How the Technique Works

Sandplay therapy is derived from Jungian analysis where specific types of play and symbols are used to interpret the child's inner life. The therapist analyzes the pictures made by the child in the sandbox and interprets what the symbols mean. It is thought that the therapist's understanding of the picture creates trust between the child and therapist similar to the bond between a mother and child (Kalff, 1980). This bond is healing in and of itself, and the therapist's interpretation generally does not need to be shared with the child. On occasion, however, it is helpful to share with the child how the picture he or she has made represents a real-life conflict. The therapist looks to the details in the picture to get a sense of what direction the therapy needs to take. The therapist is always looking toward the child's next developmental step and tries to move the child in this direction.

## Definition

Sandplay therapy is a therapeutic tool where the arrangement of small toys and objects in a sandbox is used to interpret unconscious symbols and processes. Sandplay therapy was conceived in England by Margaret Lowenfeld. The concept was developed into a therapeutic technique by Charlotte Buhler, who gathered the materials needed for the technique into a package that clinicians could purchase. Buhler brought sandplay therapy to the United States, while Jungian analyst Dora Kalff taught the technique in other parts of the world. A native of Switzerland, Kalff's widespread travels and lectures popularized the technique throughout the world.

## Indicators/Measures of Success

The success of this type of therapy is frequently measured by an
anecdotal log. However, it would be better measured by the frequent
administration of a symptom checklist.

## Suggested Readings and Resources

Kalff, D. *Sandplay.* Boston: Sigo Press, 1980.

Technique

# Self-Calming Techniques

## When to Use the Technique

Children who have trouble with anger control can benefit from this technique.

## Patient Age and Profile

Children and adolescents of all ages can learn these techniques and use them effectively.

## How the Technique Works

All relaxation techniques have the same physiological result: decreased muscle tension, lower pulse and blood pressure, slower breathing, and a brainwave pattern predominated by alpha waves. Once self-calming techniques have been learned and practiced, many children can induce relaxation in just a few moments. Being able to achieve this lowered state of physiological readiness not only inhibits the child's aggressive impulse but also increases self-esteem (by increasing the child's sense of self-control).

It is much easier to teach children anger control when you can provide them with an alternative for their current inappropriate behavior. Self-calming techniques are most effective when introduced at a time when the child and therapist have established a working relationship, and there is at least some motivation to learn these new skills. These techniques will likely not be effective unless the child sees that they are in his or her best interest to learn them.

The first step in teaching self-calming techniques is to help children identify incidences when they are likely to feel more "wound-up." Children should try to find a word that describes how they feel just before they have an angry outburst or aggressive response. Some children describe themselves as "upset," "stressed-out," "ready to explode," and so on.

The therapist should help the child choose a word that is descriptive of the child's emotional and physical state rather than words that describe the unwanted behavior. For example, if children describe their feelings

### Definition

Self-calming techniques include a variety of relaxation-training techniques, designed to help children lower their body-arousal state when they feel that they are likely to act out aggressively.

with phrases such as, "I feel like I could kill some-body," they should be encouraged to think of alternative ways to describe their feelings of tension, rather than having them describe an unwanted action.

Once a child has been able to name the feeling that precedes an emotional outburst, the child must learn to recognize the internal and external cues that are associated with that state.

The following techniques have proven helpful in teaching angry children to calm themselves down:

1. *Deep breathing.* This is the simplest technique to teach children. Make it more significant by telling the child that many admired figures—athletes, rock stars, pilots—use the same method when they need to calm down.

First ask the child to be aware of his or her breathing by placing a hand on the child's diaphragm. Then suggest that the child breathe in deeply through the nose so that the stomach and then the chest expands, as if a balloon were being blown up inside. Tell the child to slowly let the air out.

This technique is usually introduced while the child is sitting or reclining, but it should also be practiced while the child is standing or engaged in an activity, since this represents the more likely posture the child would have when he or she needs to calm down.

2. *Music therapy.* Music can also be an aid to teaching children relaxation techniques. Classical or other forms of soothing music can be an adjunct to other relaxation techniques or work by themselves. Adults trying to help an angry or aggressive child should be aware of the stress effects of noise on increasing a child's arousal state.

Just as soothing music can produce a relaxed physiological state, loud and random noise has been shown to be a significant stressor. Although children and teenagers may prefer blaring stereos and the TV at high volume, they should be made aware of the physiological effects of loud noise as they learn to control their tempers and behaviors.

3. *Visualization.* Having children visualize themselves in a relaxing scene can take many forms, from an elaborate guided tour the child can take under the therapist's direction to a very simple visualization of an everyday act.

Children should be given the choice of either keeping their eyes open or shutting them to create a visual image (many children will be uncomfortable shutting their eyes with the therapist present, making it hard for them to relax). The following are some of the more popular visualization techniques:

- Ask the child to imagine descending a stairway of 20 steps. Starting at the top, the child is instructed to relax a bit more as he or she slowly goes down each step.

- Have the child count backwards from 10 and relax a little more with each succeeding number.

- Have the child visualize ten candles being blown out, one by one. The child relaxes with each exhalation until the room is dark.

- Suggest that the child stare at a point on the wall and imagine leaves falling one at a time from that point to the floor. As each leaf falls, the child feels more relaxed.

- Have the child imagine a hot-air balloon weighted down by heavy sandbags, each of which represents a problem. Have the child visualize the bags dropping off, one by one, until the balloon floats freely and can go to a special place. The child can stay in that special place until he or she is ready to return.

## Indicators/Measures of Success

When the child is able to calm down without expressing any aggressive feelings, the self-calming technique can be considered successful.

## Forms

To use self-calming techniques effectively, children must first learn to identify situations that precede angry outbursts or aggressive encounters. The Anger Thermometer (page 187) is a chart that the child can use to identify the situations that raise him or her to the boiling point as well as situations (or people or things) that help calm him or her down. See also the Relaxation Chart on page 207.

## Suggested Readings and Resources

Hart, A. *Stress and Your Child.* Dallas: Word Publishers, 1992.

Moser, A. *Don't Pop Your Cork on Mondays!* Kansas City, MO: Landmark Editions, 1988.

Shapiro, L., and L. Slap-Shelton. *Take a Deep Breath: The Kids' Play-Away Stress Book.* King of Prussia, PA: The Center for Applied Psychology, 1992.

# Self-Monitoring

## When to Use the Technique

This technique can be used effectively in reducing nearly any targeted behavior, assuming that the child has the ability to control the behavior and is sufficiently motivated to so do.

## Patient Age and Profile

This technique can be used with children as young as 5 years old. The type of monitoring system will vary according to the child's age. For example, a 5 year old might put a check on a chart when performing a chore; a 7 year old might put a chip in a jar every time he or she hears a chime go off while doing homework; a teenager might use a wrist counter to note how often he or she makes an assertive statement in class or at home.

## How the Technique Works

In behavioral terms, it is assumed that self-monitoring can lead to self-reinforcement, and thus dysfunctional or undesirable behaviors can be changed into more appropriate ones. In many cases, simply being able to control the symptom may in itself be sufficient reward to change a behavior.

## Indicators/Measures of Success

The success of this technique can be measured by recording the change in the targeted behavior.

## Suggested Readings and Resources

Jones, V. *Adolescents with Behavior Problems*. Boston: Allyn and Bacon, 1980.

### Definition

Self-monitoring is a technique in which children observe and monitor their targeted behavior, which contributes to an identified problem. Self-monitoring can also be used to gather a baseline for other forms of treatment. Additionally, it can be used as a way of redirecting a child's attention. It is not unusual for behavior to change as a result of simply increasing one's self-awareness of it. The therapist can learn a lot about a child based upon the child's self-observation and following report. The child can use the technique to identify stressors in his or her life, and distortions in the child's perceptions can be identified by the therapist.

Technique

# Solutions Tic-Tac-Toe

### When to Use the Technique

The ICPS techniques (see below) have been particularly effective with impulsive and aggressive children.

### Patient Age and Profile

This technique can be used with children as young as 5 years old.

### How the Technique Works

This is a simple game developed for the I Can Problem Solve (ICPS) program by Myrna Shure and David Spivak. It is used to help young children see how easy it is to generate alternative solutions to a problem, rather than squabble or fight over it.

### Indicators/Measures of Success

Changes in behavior can be measured formally with a standardized behavioral checklist or informally by keeping track of how many times the techniques are used spontaneously by the children involved in the program.

### Suggested Readings and Resources

Shure, M. *Raising a Thinking Child.* New York: Henry Holt, 1994.

---

## Definition

One of the simplest and most effective games to teach problem solving is called "Solutions Tic-Tac-Toe." When a conflict arises, the two people sit down and play a game of Tic-Tac-Toe, with the additional rule being that when an X or an O is written down, the player must come up with a new and reasonable solution to the problem at hand. After ten different solutions are given, the players simply decide which one is the best. If no solution can be agreed upon, the play begins again.

# Special Time

## When to Use the Technique

Special time may be used with children who have problem behaviors, oppositional defiant disorder, and ADHD. This intervention, which can also be used to strengthen the parent-child relationship, is also used in parent-child interaction therapy.

## Patient Age and Profile

Children and parents of all ages can benefit from this technique.

## How the Technique Works

Children who exhibit problem behaviors typically receive disproportionately high amounts of criticism and other negative feedback from their environment. Although such negative feedback can reduce the number of incidents of misbehavior among other children, these youngsters are much less likely to respond in socially acceptable ways. Parents need to remember that such children don't misbehave to spite their parents; they lack the ability to behave.

Too often, children are at the receiving end of commands, directives, and ultimatums. Special time is the time when they are in control, and it gives children a sense of confidence, competence, and security.

The "who, what, when, where, and why" of special time are described as follows:

**Who.** Special time is time reserved for the child and parent. Although it is possible that both parents can be involved in the same special time, it is preferable that each parent engage the child in his or her own special time. This allows the parent more opportunity to practice ignoring misbehavior and focus on the positive. It also allows for more interaction between parent and child, further strengthening the individual parent-child relationship.

**What.** During special time, the child is boss. He or she sets the agenda and is free to engage in whatever (safe) activity is desired. This can involve any activity, from reading aloud to playing football to watching TV. Preferably, the special time activity will be an active engagement between the parent and the child.

### Definition

Special time is a specified allotment of time for the child and parent to be alone together. During this time the parent should not issue any corrective, critical, or disparaging remarks. The child chooses an activity to engage in with the parent, and the parent offers only positive reinforcement. Specifically, special time teaches the parent ignoring skills and to focus more on positive behavior, helps the parent develop a positive attitude toward the child, shifts focus from the child's weaknesses to the child's strengths, increases the child's feelings of self-worth by reducing the amount of criticism and negative feedback received, and strengthens the parent-child relationship.

**When.** Parents should first explain the concept of special time to the child. When the child is clear as to what it is and what the ground rules are, the parent and child should agree on what time is a good time for special time. Special time is ideally scheduled at the same time each day. It should last approximately 10 to 20 minutes.

**Where.** It is difficult to determine a set location for special time, as the location must be context-appropriate with the child's chosen activity. Special time can also be designated at school to provide a more positive relationship between the child and teacher, although the child's choice of activities must, of course, be more limited.

**Why.** As stated previously, special time is a time when the child is the boss. In addition to providing the child with a sense of power, special time teaches adults how to ignore bad behavior and to focus on the positive. In doing so, it also strengthens the adult-child relationship. Having special time with parents and other important adults is an effective way to improve a child's self-concept.

During special time, the parent may be annoyed by the child's misbehaviors. It is important, however, that the parent remain nondirective, uncritical, and accepting. Special time is supposed to foster ignoring and positive thinking; parents defeat the purpose of special time if they break this promise.

A parent should only intervene when the child is about to engage in something that is potentially dangerous. With some forethought, these dangers can be eliminated (i.e., by removing breakable objects from a play area). By using preventive intervention (see the section in this book on preventive intervention), the parent can remain uncritical and nondirective and uphold the ground rules of special time, intervening only to ensure safety.

There are really no reasons not to use special time. Special time should not be contingent on a child's behavior or academic progress. It is not a reward but a way to build a child's long-term self-image and to boost the parent-child relationship. It is an especially powerful intervention. Although parents often stop using many behavior-management programs in the home (they may become discouraged, for instance), they tend to continue using special time. Parents should always remember that special time is not "just playing" but rather a valuable and important therapeutic intervention.

## Indicators/Measures of Success

When the child and parent spend an enjoyable, measured amount of "quality" time together, the goal of special time will have been achieved.

## Suggested Readings and Resources

Hembree-Kigin, T., and C. B. McNeil. *Parent-Child Interaction Therapy.* New York: Plenum, 1995.

Technique

# Squiggle/Scribble Technique

## When to Use the Technique

This art technique is useful for resistant children, children who are shy about speaking, or victims of child or sexual abuse. It is particularly useful for children who resist other drawing techniques because of their self-consciousness about their artistic ability.

## Patient Age and Profile

Young children and their families can benefit from this technique.

## How the Technique Works

This game helps build rapport with the child, furnishes the therapist with valuable information about the child's inner world, and provides opportunities to indirectly offer children new ideas or solutions to their problems. Selekman (1997) includes the parents in this technique, having them draw a squiggle, after which the child constructs a picture out of it and tells a story about what he or she drew. The child then draws a squiggle, and the parents follow the same procedure.

Variations: A group of children or a family take turns drawing a common picture using crayons, pencils, or other colorful drawing instruments. The first person makes a scribble and each person in turn adds to the picture with another scribble. This continues until the group reaches a consensus that the picture is complete. The counselor then leads a discussion regarding what the picture shows and what the group process revealed.

Both the counselor and the therapist draw a scribble or squiggle on individual pieces of paper. They then exchange papers and complete a drawing based on the other person's squiggle. Both drawings are then subject to discussion and interpretation as to their projective meaning.

This technique is also effective with soft clay.

## Indicators/Measures of Success

When both child and parent have drawn a meaningful picture from a squiggle and are able to discuss it, the technique is successful.

### Definition

This play therapy technique is easy to use and fun for children. The essence of the technique is to draw a picture using a scribble as a starting place. Variations of this technique can be used as a way to develop rapport with individual children or as a projective technique to gain insight. As a group technique, the therapist introduces this as a "game," where everyone in the group will add to a group drawing.

## Suggested Readings and Resources

Winnicott, D. *Playing and Reality*. New York: Basic Books, 1971.

# Storytelling Techniques

## When to Use the Technique

Storytelling techniques, both oral and written, have been increasingly recommended for use with angry or difficult children. Although nearly all therapists and counselors apply behavioral techniques to deal with dysfunctional behaviors of angry children, they should not neglect techniques that deal with the intrapsychic and developmental aspects of the anger.

## Patient Age and Profile

Young children can benefit most from this technique.

## How the Technique Works

Dr. Richard A. Gardner suggests that children with severe behavior problems such as conduct disorders are deficient in their sense of guilt about their behavior, and that one goal of therapy is to literally make a child feel more guilty. (In psychoanalytic terms, this would be referred to as enhancing super-ego controls.)

Gardner is the originator of the mutual storytelling technique, which was designed to help therapists communicate to children on a metaphoric level. Gardner stresses the power of fables and stories in shaping the behavior of people within a particular culture (i.e., the Bible is essentially a collection of stories that people use to guide behavior and form their ethics and values).

The mutual storytelling technique begins with the child randomly selecting a stimulus object and then telling a story about it. For example, one of Gardner's early storytelling games, "The Bag of Toys," has children pick from a bag of small toys, which includes animals, people, common objects, monsters, and so on. The child then goes on to tell a story about the toy and draw a lesson or moral from the story.

To encourage the child to play the game, the child can win one chip for the toy and two chips for telling the lesson. The therapist then picks a toy and tells a corrective story, using a similar theme, but has the protagonist act in ways that are more realistic, which show better coping

### Definition

Stories are a way of communicating with children on a metaphoric level, and as such are able to give indirect messages that children might reject off-handedly with more direct approaches. Storytelling techniques can take many forms, but they share in common the objectification of the problem by placing it on "someone else." When children hear, read, or write about other children (or animals) who have problems with anger control, they can more easily communicate about the various aspects of this problem and can more readily see solutions.

skills, and which show personal responsibility. This technique can continue over many sessions, with the therapist addressing the developmental aspects of the child's problems through metaphoric messages.

Written stories developed by the therapist and the child can also be an effective way of helping children deal with intrapsychic and developmental issues. Written stories draw on the techniques of bibliotherapy, as the therapist and child conjointly write a "book" dealing with a fictional character with problems similar to the child in therapy. In writing the book, the therapist can direct the child to finding solutions to the protagonist's problems that can be used by the child in his or her own life. Children can draw illustrations to go with the story, take Polaroid pictures, or even use computer "clip-art."

Gardner has devised a variety of games that make the mutual storytelling technique more inviting to children, including published games such as "Dr. Gardner's Pick-and-Tell Games" and games that use common objects easily made by the therapist. The Bag of Words in "Dr. Gardner's Pick-and-Tell Games," for example, uses 50 or more small cards with individual emotionally evocative words printed on them. In working around the issues of anger control, the therapist might include words such as: "guilty," "bad," "hit," "bruise," "jail," "conscience," "cry," "blood," and so on. The child then reaches into the bag, picks a word, tells a story using that word as a jumping-off point, then draws a lesson or moral from the story. The therapist does the same.

Gardner has also applied a variation of this technique in rewriting common fairy tales. Instead of problems being solved by magic and wishes, the protagonist succeeds by problem-solving, personal accountability, and reality-based decisions (for example, instead of waiting for Prince Charming to come to her house with the glass slipper, Cinderella joins a dating service and picks out her own mate).

Rewriting fairy tales is also an interesting exercise for children to see the results of problem-solving and realistic (as opposed to magical) thinking. To use this technique, the therapist has the child dictate a favorite fairy tale as he or she remembers it and records it as the child speaks, using a new page for each new plot element. The therapist then rewrites the story on the bottom of each page, modernizing it by using a child of the same age as the patient or protagonist. The story should be resolved through the positive efforts and attributes of the protagonist, which should be similar to those attributes possessed by the patient.

## Indicators/Measures of Success

When children can effectively communicate the various aspects of their problems and more readily see solutions as a result of this technique, it can be considered successful.

## Suggested Readings and Resources

Gardner, R. *Conduct Disorders of Childhood.* Cresskill, NJ: Creative Therapeutics, 1994.

_____. *Dr. Gardner's Pick-and-Tell Games.* Cresskill, NJ: Creative Therapeutics, 1994.

_____. *Modern Fairy Tales for Today's Children.* Cresskill, NJ: Creative Therapeutics, 1977.

_____. *The Psychotherapeutic Techniques of Dr. Richard A. Gardner* (rev. ed.). Cresskill, NJ: Creative Therapeutics, 1992.

# Stress Inoculation

## When to Use the Technique

Adults working with angry, defiant, or difficult children should work to reduce as many stressors in the child's life as possible, even those which the child might not identify as stress (i.e., too much TV, loud music, too much junk food, etc.). Children may have stress from internal sources (i.e., anxiety, learning problems, a predisposition to impulsivity) or from external sources (i.e., a divorce, a chaotic home, a deprived environment).

## Patient Age and Profile

Children of all ages can be helped by this technique.

## How the Technique Works

Stress can be an important contributor to the behavior and emotional liability of children. Stress inoculation training involves these major components:

1. *Generalized exposure to stress.* Some parents try to protect their children from stress and stressful situations. They feel that childhood should be a "protected state" and that children will have to deal with problems soon enough. Parents with angry or impulsive children may tend to overprotect their children, trying to keep them from "going-off."

Although both of the above rationales have some validity, parents must also realize that children need to learn to deal with stress as a part of their emotional growth. Hart (1992) suggests a variety of ways to gradually expose children to stress so that they can build up the appropriate coping mechanisms:

- Tell children the truth about family problems in simplified and age-appropriate ways.

- Let children know that there are real problems in the world, allowing them to help those in need.

- Give children responsibilities that will challenge their resourcefulness.

- Allow children to solve their own problems—first simple ones, then more complex ones.

---

### Definition

Stress inoculation is an intervention designed to teach children adaptive methods of coping with stress-producing situations. The focus is not on eliminating stress but on teaching the child to learn to identify and cope with it in a more effective manner. The term "stress inoculation" assumes that children can be "inoculated" to deal with stress, much the way they can be inoculated against a virus when it is likely they will be exposed to that virus.

---

- Allow children to experience the "negative" emotions that accompany problems (i.e., if a pet dies, don't rush out to replace it, but rather allow time for the mourning process).

- Teach children to allow themselves adequate time for recovery from too much stress.

- Teach children to filter stressors. Some children have the same reaction to minor and major problems. Children can learn to recognize unimportant problems or stressors and not react to them.

2. *The identification of specific stressors.* It is important to identify all of the stresses in a child's life. Stress has a cumulative effect, and a large number of minor stresses can have the same effect as a major stressful event.

3. *The identification of specific techniques to reduce stress.* There are many techniques that can be used to help children learn to both reduce stress and cope with it, such as:

- *The Stress Diary.* The Stress Diary is a daily record of specific things that stress the child and a record of how he or she deals with those stressors. When an adult takes the time on a daily basis to talk to the child about what has bothered him or her and what can be done about it, that time is itself a stress-reduction technique. In addition, the Stress Diary also reveals patterns and suggests new ways to successfully respond to stress.

- *Cognitive interventions.* For angry or aggressive children, one technique is to see their angry or aggressive behavior as a stressor itself. The inappropriate or chronic expression of anger or aggression almost always brings about a negative reaction from others, leading to more stress for the child.

One cognitive technique used with children is to see this problem as "outside" the child. Some therapists identify the "angry monster" that needs to be tamed, emphasizing that this is something apart from the child's personality that can changed. The therapist can then form a "battle plan" with the child to fight the angry monster.

Older children can be helped to see the "cognitive distortions" or "irrational thinking" that is behind much of their acting-out behaviors. For example, the child who continually gets into trouble in school for wrestling in line with the boy in front of him explains, "Mike always starts it. He grabs me, and then I have to fight him." This child can be helped to see that his fighting is in part caused by his behavior as well as the other boy's. In addition, even if the other boy provokes him, the first child doesn't have to respond by fighting.

- *Using self-talk.* Children can also be taught to use positive self-talk as a way of learning to control their anger. This technique has children reenact situations that led to their angry outbursts and aggressions, but they "talk to themselves" while they do it, as if there were a wise owl sitting on their shoulders telling them what to do.

Positive self-talk can be effective in teaching children to "think before they act" as well as in developing a variety of coping skills to deal with stress. It should be noted, however, that this technique requires considerable practice with the therapist or counselor before it can be used effectively in the child's natural environment. Videotaping the child practicing positive self-talk and then showing him or her the tape is also recommended as a way of teaching this new behavior.

- *Relaxation.* Relaxation or self-calming techniques can also be effective in dealing with specific stressors. These techniques include deep breathing, muscle relaxation, and imagery.

## Indicators/Measures of Success

When the child is able to better handle the various stressors in his or her life, this technique can be considered successful.

## Forms

Children's Stress Scale, pages 191-195.

## Suggested Readings and Resources

Hart, A. *Stress and Your Child.* Dallas: Word Publishers, 1992.

Shapiro, E., and C. Cole. *Behavior Change in the Classroom.* New York: The Guilford Press, 1994.

Technique

# Structural Family Therapy

The structural approach is most closely identified with Salvador Minuchin and his colleagues, including Braulio Montalvo, Harry Aponte, Jay Haley, Edgar Auerswald, Lynn Hoffman, and Charles Fishman.

The primary goal of structural family therapy is to create organizational change within the family. Sherman and Fredman (1986) outline the ways that structural techniques can help a family to reorganize their system:

1. *Create movement.* Clients are generally stuck in their present way of thinking and operating and do not know how to change. A structural change in the family shifts the habitual patterns and encourages further movement. For example, disengaging a child from a parental role may allow a less-involved parent to step forward and assume more leadership.

2. *Change perspectives.* When family members assume new positions within the family, they are given the chance to observe things from a different perspective. This new perspective may allow the family members to understand the situation in a new way.

3. *Shift distribution of power.* The therapist can align himself or herself with different subsystems in the family. This serves to give more authority to the subsystem, which can break up inequities and deadlocks. For example, the therapist might back up the parents' role of making rules for the children or help draw a stronger boundary between a couple and an overinvolved in-law.

4. *Disrupt coalitions.* The therapist can work to break up inappropriate combinations. For example, one parent and a child may combine in opposition to the other parent. When the child is removed from this interaction, the bond between the parents is re-established.

5. *Form new alliances.* New, appropriate coalitions can be formed within the family. For example, if the parents have not been working together, they can be coached on ways to work together as an effective parenting unit.

## Definition

Structural family therapy is one of the most prominent models in use today. The basic premise of the model is that an individual's symptoms can only be understood as part of the family's structural pattern. The symptom is seen as a system regulator, diverting attention away from other, more basic family conflicts. In order to alleviate the symptom, a change in the family structure must first take place. As the structure of the family changes, the underlying hidden conflict can be addressed, and the need for the symptom is eliminated.

6. *Clarify boundaries between and among the subsystems.* Boundaries that are too rigid can be made more flexible, and boundaries that are too loose can be tightened up. The therapist can help the family define who should be included in what function and who should take on what responsibilities. The family may need guidance in fostering more sharing and cooperation.

7. *Discover new aspects of self.* Structural shifts may allow members to try out new behaviors and discover different aspects of themselves. For example, a too-serious family member may be put in charge of family fun, and an unreliable person might be given more responsibility.

8. *Normalize the feeling experience.* Family members may be judging themselves negatively for the role they have taken on within the system. The therapist can validate and normalize this experience to reduce feelings of being bad, unworthy, or powerless. For example, the therapist might say, "In your situation, I'd feel depressed (angry, hurt, etc.) also."

9. *Reframe the meaning of a particular role.* Family members may need help in seeing the benefit of the role they play. For example, an eldest child who complains of the responsibility might be told that this responsibility will prepare him or her to be a leader later in life.

10. *Change the family system while working with one individual.* Changing the position of one person might very well change the structure of the rest of the family. The therapist can help an individual to change, which will force the rest of the family to realign. This is especially helpful with families who resist or refuse to come in regularly for therapy as a family unit.

## When to Use the Technique

Structural family therapy has been used for virtually all problems that families face, and its techniques have been integrated into other forms of therapy as well. This type of therapy seems to be particularly relevant where the problematic behaviors can clearly be resolved by a significant family effort, such as with eating disorders, conduct disorders, drug and alcohol abuse, and so on.

## Patient Age and Profile

This system of therapy can be helpful with all families and children of any age.

## How the Technique Works

This theory of change is based on a systemic/ecological view of human behavior, namely that every microculture is derived from the specific needs within that culture, and that the system strives to maintain itself against all change (homeostasis). In theory, interrupting the factors that maintain homeostasis will cause an altering of the system to a healthier form, which in turn will solidify into a more functional system.

## Indicators/Measures of Success

This technique can be judged successful when the presenting symptoms have been objectively alleviated, as well as when the family subjectively feels that there is an improvement in family communication.

## Suggested Readings and Resources

Sherman, R., and N. Fredman. *Handbook of Structured Techniques in Marriage and Family Therapy.* New York: Brunner/Mazel, 1986.

# Theraplay

Theraplay is a time-limited therapy that starts with an assessment session based on activities similar to those offered during treatment. This helps the therapist better understand where there are specific interaction deficits between parent and child. The first four half-hour sessions are spent with the parent observing the interaction between therapist and patient, as the former creates a nonverbal climate of play and delight. In the last four sessions, the parent is invited into the room for the last fifteen minutes to join in with the child in a new way.

## When to Use the Technique

Theraplay was designed for children who have been disadvantaged when it comes to receiving adequate parenting. Children who do not meet their parents' needs, who might never have adequately bonded with their parents, or children who took care of the parent are all good candidates for theraplay. These children might bring presenting complaints of depression, withdrawal, aggression, and psychosomatic symptoms or hyperactivity.

## Patient Age and Profile

Theraplay is most often practiced with children between 6 months and 10 to 11 years. Because theraplay intervenes at a preverbal level, this approach is well suited to children without good verbal skills, overactive children, or overintellectualized children. Any child who would benefit from a very hands-on, highly interactive, enjoyable approach will gain from theraplay.

## How the Technique Works

There are two basic principles to theraplay: (1) The adult is in charge, and (2) it should be fun. These principles grow out of the basic assumption of theraplay, which is to recreate the special, highly charged, lovingly playful atmosphere of parents with infants. This attempt to re-parent or at least rebond, both gives the child some new growth-producing experiences and models empathy, parental control, and parental delight in one's offspring. The child's sense of being a worthwhile human being is further strengthened by the new relationship between the parent and child.

### Definition

Theraplay was devised to provide a second parenting experience for children who may not have had adequate parenting initially. Theraplay strives to give children positive parenting experiences in a lively, physical, personal, and engaged way. It is an attempt to offer poorly bonded parents and children a second chance by re-enacting some of the most delightful early parent-infant activities. These activities fall into five general categories: structuring, challenging, intruding/exciting, nurturing, and playfulness.

## Indicators/Measures of Success

Success in theraplay is measured by the child's greater willingness to share, an enhanced capacity for pleasure and fun, as well as a greater sense of trust. Increased parental involvement in play and fun with the child, and greater parental control and child responsiveness are also indicators of success.

## Suggested Readings and Resources

Jernberg, A. *Theraplay: A Structured New Approach for Problem Children and Their Families.* San Francisco: Jossey-Bass, 1979.

Marschak, M. *Parent-Child Interaction and Youth Rebellion.* New York: Gardner, 1980.

Weston, D. *Playful Parenting: Turning the Dilemma of Discipline into Fun & Games.* Los Angeles: Teacher/Pedigree, 1993.

# Time-out

## When to Use the Technique

Time-out is the most common form of discipline for virtually any kind of child misbehavior.

## Patient Age and Profile

Time-out is an effective intervention for children between the ages of 18 months and 10 years. When used correctly, it is a highly effective method for reducing incidents of problematic behavior.

## How the Technique Works

Time-out may be chosen over other types of consequences because (1) acting-out children are motivated to avoid it because it keeps them from stimulating activities, including getting attention from others; (2) nothing is more punishing to young children than complete boredom; (3) unlike some other consequences (i.e., restriction of privileges), time-out can occur within seconds of the inappropriate behavior; (4) unlike spanking, short time-outs can be safely administered numerous times a day, thereby allowing the parent to be more consistent in following through with consequences; (5) it does not usually cause children to become more aggressive; and (6) it is the most commonly used discipline strategy in preschool and elementary school classrooms. Use at home will promote greater cross-setting consistency and enhance the child's behavioral adjustment at school as well as at home.

In addition to serving as an instructional tool, time-out also serves as an effective deterrent to repeating similar problematic behavior in the future. The child learns to associate time-out as an aversive consequence to specific misbehavior. Since time-out does not entail physical or verbal abuse or other negative treatment to the child, the parent-child relationship is unthreatened.

Time-out should be used to discipline only the child's most serious misbehaviors. It is undesirable to generalize time-out's aversive consequences to many behaviors, weakening the specific association intended to be established between time-out and the problematic behavior. If the child knows that hitting a sibling will lead to time-out

### Definition

Time-out is an extreme form of ignoring, in which the noncompliant child is removed from all sources of positive reinforcement. It is a relatively simple method of discipline that is an effective substitute for other methods of parental discipline, such as criticizing, hitting, and yelling. Further, it allows the parent to avoid responding to the child in anger.

(because the parent has exclusively paired time-out with this behavior), the child will be likely to think twice before hitting the sibling in the future.

In general, a parent using time-out will (1) tell the child the specific misbehavior at issue, and (2) instruct the child to go to a time-out center (a boring, low-stimulation area, usually a corner). The purpose of the time-out center is to remove the child from the problem situation and allow him or her the opportunity to cool off and think about the misbehavior. The child is then allowed to return to whatever he or she was doing and have another opportunity to behave in an appropriate manner.

Before implementing time-out, the parent and child should sit down together and discuss what time-out is and for which behaviors it will be used. Parents should be specific and thorough. It is important that the child understand the consequences that will follow misbehavior. Be sure to explain exactly how time-out works:

- A timer at the time-out center will be set for the recommended time.

- The child will sit in the time-out chair for the designated period of time.

- If the child gets up before the designated period of time, the timer will be reset, with an extra minute added, and the child will have to sit down again.

- At the end of the time-out, the child will be free to leave.

Immediately after the child misbehaves, he or she should be alerted to this fact and sent to time-out. A simple, specific, and clear statement should be used. For example: "Jay, you kicked the dog again. This is against the rules, so you have to go to time-out." Make sure that the specific misbehavior is stated. It is also important that the punishment be immediate and used consistently. Do not engage the child in conversation or succumb to delaying statements.

The site chosen for the time-out center is important. The center should include a chair and should be a quiet spot in a hallway or corner, away from TV, toys, and other enjoyable recreational items. The center should not be dark, scary, dangerous, or dirty. The most important quality of a time-out center is that it be boring. A timing device (a kitchen timer, or time-out timer) should be provided to measure the time.

Another important factor to take into consideration is the amount of time set aside for time-out. Time-out sessions of longer than five minutes are not recommended. A good rule of thumb for determining time-out duration is to use the child's age as the number of minutes in time-out. This means that a 3-year-old child should receive three minutes of time-out; a 4-year-old four minutes of time-out, etc. The maximum amount of time-out assigned should not exceed five minutes.

In putting a child in a time-out corner, the parent should be forceful but not angry or violent. If the command to go to time-out is not obeyed, the parent should repeat it and add another minute to the time-out duration. Only if the noncompliance continues should the parent resort to firmly guiding or carrying the child to time-out and adding yet another minute. If the child has to be carried, the parent should hold the child facing the direction of the time-out area, away from the parent.

If the child leaves the time-out center prematurely:

- Stand behind the child and hold him or her in place.

- State that you will leave when the child is calm and ready (using a calm, firm voice).

- Avoid additional conversation and ignore outbursts, as this attention may be reinforcing. The point is to remove the child from positive reinforcement for the time being.

- Reset the clock.

- Add an additional minute (not to exceed a total of 5 additional minutes).

If the child continues to resist, time-out will probably not work unless there is a physical struggle. In this case, the parent should abandon time-out and take away a privilege instead. Although the parent may feel this is giving in, it is usually more effective than fighting with the child.

After the child has finished time-out, allow him or her to return to the original scene of the misbehavior. It may be helpful to issue positive instructions to educate the child as to how to behave better in the future. Techniques such as overcorrection may be helpful at this point as well.

When time-out doesn't seem to work, ask:

- Are the rules being consistently enforced? Time-out is not effective if it is not used consistently. The child may decide to attempt a behavior and risk punishment, especially if the risk of punishment isn't great.

- Is the child seeking negative attention for being bad? Try offering more positive reinforcement during the course of the day, so that the child doesn't feel the need to be bad to receive attention. Further, keep interaction and eye contact with the child at a minimum during time-out, to ensure that the child doesn't associate time-out with receiving attention.

- Do the rules need to be explained again? If the child is not exactly sure why he or she is in time-out, it will not be an educational experience.

- Is time-out really an aversive consequence? Does the child dislike it enough? Maybe the time-out center is a little too interesting. Is it close to the TV, a radio, a window? Make sure time-out is a boring experience.

## Indicators/Measures of Success

When the child understands the reasons for time-out and time-out is serving as an effective deterrent to repeating similar problematic behavior in the future, it can be considered a success.

## Forms

Time-Out Worksheet, page 213.

## Suggested Readings and Resources

Eastman, M., and S. C. Rozen. *Taming the Dragon in Your Child: Solutions for Breaking the Cycle of Family Anger.* New York: Wiley, 1994.

Kazdin, A. *Treatment of Antisocial Behavior in Children.* Homewood, IL: Dorsey Press, 1985.

Webster-Stratton, C., and M. Herbert. *Troubled Families, Problem Children.* New York: Wiley, 1994.

# ToughLove

As parents of three unruly children, founders Phyllis and David York were "mired in finding 'reasons' for unacceptable behavior instead of setting limits on what is unacceptable and demanding that it stop." A national movement, ToughLove runs a support network based in Doylestown, PA; there are well over 1,000 ToughLove groups throughout the United States and Canada.

## When to Use the Technique

ToughLove is a network of parents helping other parents and professionals to bring change into the lives of young persons who are "impossible, incorrigible, uncontrollable, addicted, physically or verbally abusive, in trouble in school, in trouble with the law, and/or destroying the family."

## Patient Age and Profile

ToughLove is designed for adolescents and teenagers who are "out of control."

## How the Technique Works

ToughLove is a solution that depends on parents, professionals, and other community members cooperatively rejecting destructive behavior and supporting new patterns of behavior. Parents who come to ToughLove are seeking help for a wide range of problems with their children, including running away, sexual issues, suicide, incest, drugs, alcohol, and parent abuse, all of which are responsible for or contribute in some form to the anger a child or teenager will necessarily elicit in response. These parents are often desperate to stop being controlled by their unruly children and teenagers. Parents are encouraged to stop blaming themselves for the problems of their children.

ToughLove parents literally stand in for one another when parents cannot handle emotionally charged situations concerning their own children. New ToughLove parents are assigned to another family, who set bottom-line rules for all aspects of daily family life.

**Definition**

ToughLove is a self-help program for troubled families and angry children, particularly adolescents and teenagers. Its literature states, "ToughLove is an effective self-help program for the parents of unruly young people and the professionals who work with them. It is a combination of philosophy and action which, together, can help you change and help you get control of your family again."

ToughLove has documented what it is and what it is not as the following:

- We are a support group, not a therapy group.

- We are a parent support group.

- We deal in behavior, not in emotions, even though emotions are considered and respected.

- We do not act as professional counselors.

- We have no affiliation with any religious or political group.

- We cannot give you immediate answers to your problems; what we can do is show you that you are not alone, that you have rights and worth, and you deserve to be treated with respect.

- We have a process for change that you can use as a guide. We offer supportive confrontation and selective support to help you make changes.

- We give no guarantees. We do not tell you what to do. We can give suggestions, hope, and sharing. There are no prescriptions; you make your own plans and get support from the group to follow through with your decisions.

- ToughLove does not advocate or support physical or verbal abuse.

- ToughLove does not advocate or support kicking kids out; we give our kids options that protect their safety. The reality is that they may not choose our options.

ToughLove is especially helpful for use with angry children because it works to stop the unacceptable, angry behavior while it fosters a cooperative environment and enables people to take responsibility for meeting their own needs. Its tenets are:
(1) Family problems have roots and supports in the culture. (2) Parents are people, too. (3) Parents' material and emotional resources are limited. (4) Parents and children are not equal. (5) Blaming keeps people helpless. (6) Children's behavior affects parents. Parents' behavior affects kids. (7) Taking a stand precipitates a crisis. (8) From controlled crisis comes positive change. (9) Families need to give support to and get support from their own community in order to change. (10) The essence of family life is cooperation, not togetherness.

## Indicators/Measures of Success

ToughLove solutions do not always work directly, but they at least disrupt the unconscious support of the difficult child and shake things up. Children know that changes are in the making. ToughLove is not promoted as a miracle cure, but can be an alternative for parents who have not found any other way to handle children with extreme defiant or disruptive behavior.

## Forms

To most people, ToughLove is a radical solution in that it questions the traditional boundaries of the nuclear family. It is an "intrusive" technique, and so would naturally be implemented only after many other techniques have been tried. In making a decision to recommend ToughLove, a therapist or counselor should first document that less intrusive techniques have been given a fair try. Use the History of Interventions form (page 201) to ascertain the various techniques that the parent has tried and the reason(s) why those techniques have failed.

## Suggested Readings and Resources

York, P., D. York, and T. Wachtel. *ToughLove*. New York: Double-day, 1982.

_____. *ToughLove Solutions*. New York: Doubleday, 1984.

For more information on ToughLove, write or call P.O. Box 1069, Doylestown, PA 18901; 215/348-7090.

Technique

# Transactional Analysis

## When to Use the Technique

Children who have problems with anger control will benefit from this intervention.

## Patient Age and Profile

Although some TA concepts have been used with very young children, it is most appropriate for older children and teens (12 years and older). TA teaches these patients a system to understand their feelings and behaviors in nonprofessional language, and as a result, the adolescent gains a sense of self-control and assurance.

## How the Technique Works

Although TA may be used in individual therapy, it is most effective when used as a group technique. In a group situation, the therapist or counselor can observe how group members interact, helping the individual group members compare their current feelings and behavior with situations that may have occurred in the past.

A basic concept in TA is that people are neither "good" nor "bad," but we are all "OK." This concept confronts the teenager who may tend to polarize his or her world into those "for" or "against" him or her. As Freed and Freed (1977) explain in *TA for Kids:*

"[TA will] help you feel OK. . . because you are OK and always have been. By understanding your self better, by understanding and accepting your own feelings and the feelings of other important people in your life, you will get back the good feelings about yourself you may have lost and begin to trust yourself again. When you learn this, you'll probably get along better with other people and be happier, because you'll like and trust them."

TA's building blocks are based on three ego-states that dictate the way people behave, think, and feel: Parent, Adult, and Child. The Parent ego state is a collection of attitudes, thoughts, behaviors, and feelings that a person has adopted from outside sources who served as parent figures. The Adult ego-state is a data processor that organizes information,

### Definition

Transactional analysis, or TA, is a combination of both psychoanalytic and social learning concepts. One of the basic premises of this theory is that children with dysfunctional behavior are reacting to inner "voices" rather than external reality. These "voices" are referred to as "scripts," and because they have been learned from significant people in their lives, they become incor-porated into the child's personality. TA would assume that a child with excessive and unwarranted anger would be responding to these scripts, rather than to the people and situations in every-day life.

estimates probabilities, and makes logical statements. The Child ego-state consists of feelings, thoughts, and behaviors that are typical of children and spontaneous adults.

TA teaches that the three ego-states are working simultaneously within a person, being critical and nurturing (the Parent), thinking (the Adult), and feeling (the Child). The goal is for the Adult self to find a balance between the "reckless and self-centered" Child and the "punitive, judgmental" Parent. How people use the three parts to get along better and feel better about themselves is key.

If a child or adolescent is screaming, whining, or throwing a tantrum, his or her Child state has kicked in. If he or she is scolding, shaking a finger at someone, or helping someone who is hurt, the Parent state is in effect. If he or she is trying to figure out how to solve problems, the Adult state has taken charge. In TA terms, for example, angry children and adolescents are characterized as being Child-heavy in that their Child state is in charge. When they are doing things such as fighting and insisting on doing what they want now, they are responding exclusively to the needs and demands of their Child. Ideally, there is room for all three ego-states, but it is best when the Adult is most frequently in charge, because that is the ego-state than can analyze problems and work to change them.

TA teaches that the Child is a powerful ego part. The Child often does what it wants, while the Parent is worried and the Adult is in despair over what to do. Freed and Freed describe two parts of the Child: the Natural or Free Child, and the Little Professor. The Natural Child is free to laugh, cry, giggle, sulk, be happy or afraid, to love and hate, and to play and have fun. The Little Professor is the thinking part of the Child and often acts in response to what the Child wants.

It is the Little Professor that seems to play a large part in the ego states of angry children. Angry children are likely to play certain games to get "strokes" or "warm fuzzies" when they can't get them for "just being themselves." These games are usually played over and over and always end with someone else feeling angry or hurt. Such games include:

- *Mine's Better Than Yours.* This game is played to convince others that the person should be rewarded for something.

- *Tattletale.* When a child tattles, he or she is sending the message, "Give me some strokes for obeying you," without thinking of the response it will bring from peers.

- *Why don't you—yes, but.* An example of this could be:

  *Kate:* I hate Sally. She never lets me play.
  *Teacher:* Well, why don't you ask her if you can play? Could you do that?
  *Kate:* Yes, but she'd say no.
  *Teacher:* You can't know that unless you ask her.
  *Kate:* Yes, but even if she said yes, she'd make fun of me.
  *Teacher:* Well, why don't you tell her to stop if she starts teasing you? Could you do that?
  *Kate:* Yes, but she won't listen to me.

The "game" goes on and on until the teacher gives up. The child is left with the feeling that there is no way to solve the problem.

The "Game Plan" can help children decide if they are playing TA games. They should ask themselves the following questions:

- *What keeps happening to me over and over that leaves me or someone else feeling bad?*

- *What happens next?*

- *And then what happens?*

- *How does it end?*

- *How do I feel after it ends?*

- *How might the other person feel?*

Freed and Freed suggest the following "trackdown" technique to help angry children get along with others:

1. *Determine the "hurt."* As soon as you feel uncomfortable, as soon as someone says something that annoys you, or as soon as someone does something that frightens you, you can say to yourself, "I hurt," and then immediately say, "How?" The answer to this question puts you into your Adult state.

2. *Determine which part hurts: Parent, Adult, or Child.* The answer is usually Child.

3. *Who has done it?* Ask, "Who did this to me?" The answer will be the person who hurt you (mother, father, brother, sister, friend, teacher, etc.).

4. *With what?* Their Parent, Adult, or Child? If it was a mother or father, for example, that person's Parent was probably "speaking."

5. *Why did they do it?* "Because they were afraid," or "Because they were angry," or "Because they were acting to protect me" are common reasons.

6. *What can I do now?* Do an analysis of what happened and why. This keeps you from getting angry, afraid, or sad.

7. *What can I do different later?* Avoid getting hooked into your own script or the scripts that others are following.

## Indicators/Measures of Success

When children use this technique to lessen their angry outbursts, it can be considered successful.

## Suggested Readings and Resources

Engler, J., and D. Goleman. *The Consumer's Guide to Psychotherapy.* New York: Simon & Schuster, 1992.

Freed, A., and M. Freed. *TA for Kids (and Grown-Ups Too).* Sacramento, CA: Jalmar Press, 1977.

_____. *TA for Teens and Other Important People.* Sacramento, CA: Jalmar Press, 1976.

Woollams, S., and M. Brown. *TA: The Total Handbook of Transactional Analysis.* Englewood Cliffs, NJ: Prentice-Hall, 1979.

Technique

# The "Triple A" Coping with Stress Game

## Example

A schoolmate who is a bully can be avoided most of the time. Avoiding homework because you find it difficult to concentrate, on the other hand, will only cause more stress, so this is the wrong tactic.

Loud noise is experienced by the body as a stress. Turning down the music reduces that stress.

## When to Use the Technique

Children who are experiencing a great deal of stress and those with other anxiety disorders can be helped with this game.

## Patient Age and Profile

Children ages 8 through adult can benefit from this game. Three or more players can play at one time.

## How the Technique Works

This game works by teaching children three basic coping skills.

*Game play.* Players take five index cards and write their initials on the back of each. On the front they write five different stresses (things that make them angry). The cards are shuffled together and placed in a deck, with the initials of the players on top. Each player in turn picks a card and responds to the situation described on it using one of the Triple A coping strategies. A player gets 1 point for a realistic response. If the player's own card is on top of the pile, then he or she should pick the next one. If a player can't think of one of the three A's, then he or she may ask for help. Play continues for four rounds. When the group has accumulated more than 10 points, everyone is declared a winner, and a common prize is shared.

## Indicators/Measures of Success

When children exhibit signs of being stress-free, or at least feel as through stress is less of a factor in their lives, this game will have served its purpose.

---

### Definition

The object of this game is to teach children three important and basic coping skills. The three A's of stress management stand for Avoid, Alter, and Accept:

AVOID means reducing stress by keeping it out of your life as much as possible (to the extent that avoidance doesn't cause new stress).

ALTER means changing the stress at its source.

ACCEPTING the stress means learning specific ways to build up resistance to it, while understanding that the stress itself may be around for a long time. This can be done by learning to selectively ignore it, by changing oneself to better cope with a stress that cannot be modified, or by changing one's perception of the stress.

## Suggested Readings and Resources

Shapiro, L., and L. Slap-Shelton. *Take a Deep Breath: The Kids' Play-Away Stress Book.* King of
Prussia, NJ: The Center for Applied Psychology, 1994.

Technique

# The Vacation

## Definition

The vacation is used when an overinvolved member of a family is asked to step back from the characteristic overactivity that may contribute to a power inequity. In structural family terms the enmeshed member is sent on "vacation" so that the boundary between that person and others is strengthened while weak contacts between underactive members of the family are increased.

## When to Use the Technique

Problems that stem from overinvolvement of some family members and underinvolvement of others lend themselves to this approach. Specific problems that have been dealt with by the vacation include anorexia, anxiety disorders, school phobias, psychotic episodes, and aggressive acting out.

## Patient Age and Profile

This technique is directed at family members who nag, overdo for others, or are "workaholics." Family systems that have dominating, or intrusive, members may be approached through this disarming instruction: "You have been working so hard, you really need to take a break."

With families of anorectic or schizophrenic teenagers in Italy, therapists literally instructed the parents (who were seen as having not enough time together, resulting in an overconcern with the child's problems), to go away for an hour, then an evening, then a weekend, and not tell the children where they were going. This strengthened the marriage bond, which needed support, while breaking the overconcern with a child, which was seen as contributory to symptom maintenance.

## How the Technique Works

The therapist needs to express concern for the overinvolved member and ask the person to take a break. Then the family members have to be encouraged to discuss what they might do to "pick up the slack." They are warned that it will be tough, but a game plan is devised for everyone to pull together so that the overworked person can have the vacation. The premise in this technique is that symptomatic behavior is a result of overinvolvement of some family members and underinvolvement of others. This directive strives to create a better balance.

## Indicators/Measures of Success

The family must be monitored to see if the task has been carried out. Several attempts may be necessary to get a person used to activity to "do nothing," even when they feel overstressed. New alliances are encouraged, and new behaviors are sought by everyone—the overworked and underworked. If the basic family arrangements have been altered, the technique is successful; new patterns may emerge and new behaviors take the place of old ones.

## Suggested Readings and Resources

Minuchin, S. *Families and Family Therapy.* Cambridge, MA: Harvard University Press, 1974.

_____. *Psychosomatic Families.* Cambridge, MA: Harvard University Press, 1978.

Palazzoli, S., et al. *Paradox and Counterparadox.* New York: Jason Aronson, 1978.

Technique

# Visualization

## Definition

Children are asked to imagine or to visualize a specific image or series of images ("like running a movie in your mind"). Although this technique has become somewhat of a cliché in pop-psychology books and tapes, research studies have consistently shown that visualizing can be useful as an aid to a variety of therapies. Visualization is used as part of hypnotherapy, meditation, desensitization training, pain control, diminishing perform-ance anxiety, and so on.

## Example

*Fear of dogs.* A boy visualizes himself watching a fierce dog as Superman stands next to him. The child visualizes himself approaching the dog under the watchful eye of the Man of Steel, who coaches him on how to proceed. The dog then becomes friendly, and the child is unafraid.

*Headaches.* A girl sees her headache as a pounding drum. She visualizes cool "magic" blankets being wrapped around the drum until it is muffled.

*Asthma.* A boy envisions his bronchial tubes as flat balloons. He imagines that magic pumps are placed within each balloon, which makes them expand, and breathing becomes easier.

*Test anxiety.* A girl imagines that her pencil is enchanted but loses its power if it is not directly touching the paper. The pencil talks to her and encourages her to keep trying.

## When to Use the Technique

This technique could be used as an adjunct to learning any type of social, emotional, or behavioral skill that is taught in social skills training, assertiveness training, or habit control.

## Patient Age and Profile

Visualization techniques are particularly effective with young children, because they find it easy to form clear images; however, the technique can be useful at any age.

## How the Technique Works

The mind clearly has the ability to experience images as if they were real, such as in dreams. Hundreds of studies in different areas of psychology have shown that self-initiated mental images can also be experienced by the neurological system and the body as if the images were, in fact, real.

## Indicators/Measures of Success

This technique is probably best measured by a self-report checklist. The perception of change is potentially more important than the change itself (which would be measured by an objective behavioral assessment or specific performance criteria).

## Forms

Self-Report Symptom Checklist.

## Suggested Readings and Resources

Suinn, R. "Anxiety Management Training for General Anxiety." *The Innovative Psychological Therapies: Critical and Creative Combinations.* New York: Harper & Row, 1975.

Technique

# Wilderness/ Adventure Therapy

### When to Use the Technique

Children with severe behavior problems, such as conduct disorder and oppositional defiant disorder, have benefited from these programs.

### Patient Age and Profile

Wilderness/adventure therapy is usually geared toward children ages 8 through 18.

### How the Technique Works

By the time children approach adolescence, their anger and aggressive behavior may be deeply ingrained in their personality and lifestyle. Children diagnosed as defiant or with conduct disorders may be nearly impossible to treat in individual therapy, particularly if their behavior is reinforced by a peer group exhibiting similar antisocial behavior.

One method of dealing with these children is to completely remove them from the context in which their anger has been nourished and place them in a situation where their antisocial behavior is overshadowed by the need for basic survival skills. The underlying philosophy of wilderness-training programs is that children and adolescents will relinquish antisocial and aggressive behaviors when placed in groups of their peers where skills such as prosocial values, perseverance, self-denial, and compassion are necessary to meet basic day-to-day needs. The ultimate goal is to help the older child or adolescent break out of self-defeating attitudes and perceptions.

The basic rationale for wilderness programs is that adolescents will overcome patterns of antisocial behavior when confronted with an environment that cannot be manipulated, in which real obstacles must be overcome by hard work and cooperation with others, in which adolescent actions have real-world positive or negative consequences, and in which initiative and responsible behavior lead to positive results. These programs are generally considered to be more humane and effective than traditional youth corrections programs due to their low youth-to-staff ratios, intensive involvement of staff in daily activities, opportunities for frequent informal counseling and conflict resolution,

### Definition

Wilderness youth programs are generally described in terms of a sustained course of outdoor activities involving physical challenge and perceived risk, in which adolescents and staff are required to work together. These activities provide a fertile setting for counseling and education to address the adolescents' emotional and behavioral problems.

and a physical setting that engages the interest of the youths and gives them a sense of challenge and achievement.

Programs can range from day-long excursions to those that last up to a year, and they serve almost every type of clinical adolescent population. They generally include the following elements:

- A series of incrementally more difficult challenges, which seem insurmountable or dangerous but are not really as daunting as they appear. Mastery requires group perseverance, cooperation, and creativity.

- An unfamiliar environment. This is often a wilderness environment, but it may also be an unfamiliar urban setting and may involve the challenge of working with the homeless or disabled.

- Integration of the experience. Most programs invest time in helping the students understand their experience and may employ a variety of therapeutic techniques to do so.

- Value-centered philosophy. The programs attempt through real-life experiences to develop specific values in the participants.

Wilderness therapy can result in improved social skills, self-control, and self-confidence. It may be particularly effective with adjudicated youth. The following are some of the variables that make this approach successful and may help to evaluate whether a particular client could benefit from such an intervention.

- The problems presented to the participants are designed to fit the individual's needs and capabilities.

- Problems are incremental, so confidence is built on successive achievements.

- The problems are concrete, resulting in clearly defined successes or failures.

- The problems can be solved, but success is not guaranteed. This increases motivation.

- There are real consequences for failure; the individual and the group learns to accept personal responsibility.

- The tasks are multifaceted, requiring participants to use all of their faculties—cognitive, affective, and physical.

In addition to the above, this type of program relies on group processes and the use of controlled stress to improve interpersonal skills as well as self-image.

Because programs vary widely, it is necessary to consult a local directory of human services to determine what programs are available in a given area and what populations are served. Since followup is usually done by the referring agency, it is important to choose an appropriate program and coordinate closely to ensure that the therapeutic goals and concerns will be addressed.

Wilderness therapy can be very effective in increasing a child's or adolescent's sense of mastery and self-worth; however, it will not automatically change the person's behavior in the home environment. Some kind of structured assistance is usually required for the newcomer's learning to transfer, sometimes in the form of confrontations and feedback from peers, as well as goal-setting and contracting. Preparing the child or adolescent beforehand will also help increase the effectiveness of the experience.

## Indicators/Measures of Success

The greatest challenge of adventure therapy is to successfully transfer the lessons of the wilderness experience back to the youths' everyday life in the community. When this transfer of learning occurs, the intervention can be considered successful.

## Suggested Readings and Resources

Bandoroff, S. "Wilderness-Adventure Therapy for Delinquent and Pre-delinquent Youth: A Review of the Literature." *ERIC Document* 377428, 1989.

Gass, M., ed. *Adventure Therapy: Therapeutic Applications of Adventure Programming.* Dubuque, IA: Kendall-Hunt, 1993.

Lyman, R. D., S. Prentice-Dunn, and S. Gabel, eds. *Residential and Inpatient Treatment of Children and Adolescents.* New York: Plenum Press, 1989.

Miles, J., and S. Priest, eds. *Adventure Education.* State College, PA: Venture Publishing, 1990.

# Forms

*Please feel free to xerox and use the following forms as needed.*

# The Anger Thermometer

It is important to understand what makes you "hot" and what "cools" you down. Write in the people, places, and things that make you feel mad or calm.

**People, Places, Things**

**Boiling Over**

**Steaming Hot**

**Warm**

**98.6 (Normal)**

**Cool**

**Cold**

**Frigid**

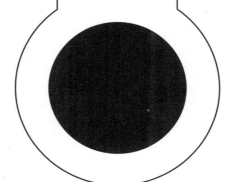

I, _____, AGREE WITH
   (NAME OF CHILD)

_____ TO _____
(PARENT OR TEACHER)    (BEHAVIOR TO CHANGE)

FOR _____
     (AMOUNT OF TIME)

IF I FULFILL THIS CONTRACT I WILL RECEIVE

_____

_____
(SIGNED)

_____
(DATE)

# BEHAVIORAL CONTRACT

I, _____, AGREE WITH
(NAME OF CHILD)

_____ TO _____
(PARENT OR TEACHER)                    (BEHAVIOR TO CHANGE)

_____ FOR _____
                                              (AMOUNT OF TIME)

IF I FULFILL THIS CONTRACT I WILL RECEIVE

_____

_____
(SIGNED)

_____
(DATE)

# The Children's Stress Scale™

*Version 1.0*

*A Rating Scale to Measure Stress On Children
and Their Ability To Cope With It*

Few people will disagree that stress is an important issue in the lives of children. Just as with adults, it is a factor in both their physical and mental health. Stress may underlie a wide assortment of common physical complaints, including headaches, stomachaches and fatigue, and may be a factor in chronic illnesses such as asthma and ulcers.

Stress can also be a predisposing factor in a range of psychological problems, including, but not Limited to, depression, academic underachievement, anxiety disorders, drug and alcohol abuse, aggression and so on. But a child under stress may not necessarily be symptomatic. In many cases severe stress can exist in children at a sub-clinical level and its toll may not show up until adolescence or even adulthood.

Identifying and understanding the stress that a child is experiencing is only half the story. What is equally important is a child's ability to cope with stress. There are many factors that can be important in how children can cope, including their inner resources, the support of their immediate family, and other environmental factors (such as school, friends, and community involvement). Therefore no two children will experience stress exactly the same way.

The Children's Stress Scale is an attempt to qualitatively measure the stress factors in a child's life as well as that child's resources in handling stress. The Children's Stress Scale was primarily designed to provide the user with intervention strategies; helping parents and professionals reduce stress and increase a child's ability to handle it. Most importantly, we hope that this scale can be an aid in making children aware of stress and helping them develop lifelong habits in dealing with it.

Child's Name _____ Age _____ Grade _____

Parent's Name _____

Primary Address and Phone # _____

_____

## Instructions

The Children's Stress Scale consists of two parts, stress factors and coping mechanisms. If you feel, because of specific factors unique to each child, that a statement should be rated higher or lower, you should feel free to add or subtract five points from that statement. Note adjustments in the column at the right with either a plus or minus sign.

Since it is impossible to list every situation or factor that affect a child's life, the adult filling out this scale should add additional statements as he/she sees fit under the section marked Other Stress Factors.

Give each Stress Factor a numerical value according to the following scale and add that number into the total Stress Score:

30     Traumatic stress factors
25     Highly significant, but not necessarily traumatic stress
20     Significant stress factors which may vary according to individual circumstances
15     Normal, but intense stress in the child's life or the family
10     Normal, but cumulative stress in the child's life
5     Low, persistent stress factors

Give each additional Coping Mechanism a score according to the following scale and add that number into the total Coping Mechanism Score:

4     Inner Resources
3     Family
2     Community

## Part I: Identifying Stress Factors

**Circle the number next to the statements below that describe the child you are rating.**

| Score | | Adjustments (+ or -5 pts) |
|---|---|---|
| 30 | The child's parents have been separated/divorced for a period of less than one year. | _____ |
| 30 | The child's parents are actively fighting over a significant issue in the child's life (this could be a custody or visitation issue, but it could also include such issues as where to go to school, a discipline issue, etc.). | _____ |
| 30 | A member of the child's immediate family has died within the past year (father, mother, sibling, or a significant other with whom the child spent more than ten hours a week). | _____ |
| 30 | The child has experienced a natural disaster within the past 12 months, including: fire, earthquake, flooding, and so on. | _____ |
| 30 | The child frequently uses "drugs" including alcohol, illegal substances, as well as cigarette and the abuse of vitamins, diet pills, and so on. | _____ |
| 30 | The child's family has moved more than 100 miles away. | _____ |
| 30 | The child has had to switch schools. | _____ |

30    The child has experienced a recent separation, with limited contact, from one parent due to military duty, job relocation, or other external factors.    _____

30    One or both of the child's parents has remarried within the past year (this situation can be more stressful depending on many factors including the presence of step-siblings, the child's relationship with the step-parent, and so on).    _____

30    The child has experienced a prolonged illness (more than 1 month) and/or hospitalization.    _____

30    The child occasionally uses "drugs" including alcohol and illegal substances, as well as cigarette and the abuse of vitamins, diet pills, and so on.    _____

30    The family income has been substantiallY reduced in the past six months.    _____

25    The child is experiencing a prolonged period of difficulties in school.    _____

20    The child is experiencing significant problems with his/her peers, including, but not limited to: prolonged teasing or harassment, social ostracism, aggression to or from peers, etc.    _____

20    The child perceives that he/she is significantly different than his/her close peers (due to physical differences, ethnic or racial differences, language differences, learning differences, and so on).    _____

20    One or more of a child's parents has a significant or chronic physical or mental illness.    _____

15    The parents of a child are experiencing prolonged and obvious problems including: frequent quarreling, problems at work, problems with relatives, health-related problems, etc.    _____

15    The child is entering a new school as part of his/her normal school career (e.g., preschool to elementary school, elementary to middle school, etc.)    _____

15    The child is in a disadvantaged environment (e.g., the family's income is below the poverty line and/or the child is exposed to significant social problems).    _____

15    Expectations for the child are significantly unrealistic concerning his/her innate abilities.    _____

10    The child is having a significant reaction to local or world events (e.g., The Persian Gulf War caused fears and anxiety in a significant number of the nation's children. Local or regional news about violence may have a similar effect on some children.).    _____

10    The child's week is "over-scheduled," so that nearly every day he/she is running from one activity to another (a "hurried" child).    _____

5    There is a general lack of organization and scheduling in the household.    _____

5    The child does not have a nutritious, well-balanced diet.    _____

5    The child is entering a new school year.    _____

5    The child watches television and/or plays video games for more than two hours a day.    _____

5    The child is exposed to long periods of high decibel noise.    _____

*Other Stress Factors* (please fully describe and enter an appropriate numerical rating of 30, 25, 20, 10, or 5)

_____

_____

_____

_____

Total Score _____

Plus or Minus Adjustments _____

Final Stress Factors Score _____

# Part II: Coping Mechanisms

Circle the numbers by the statements that accurately describe the child whom you are rating from an age-appropriate perspective.

Score

Adjustments
(+ or -5 pts)

## Inner Resources:

4    The child readily communicates his/her feelings.    _____

4    The child has hobbies or interests (other than school work) which he/she spends time
     with each week.    _____

4    The child has excellent study and organizational skills.    _____

4    The child actively seeks out adult help when needed.    _____

4    The child actively seeks out peer help for support when needed.    _____

4    The child has a resilient personality and even-tempered disposition.    _____

4    The child adapts particularly well to transitions.    _____

4    The child has an exceptional striving towards independence.    _____

## Family:

3    The child has specific time each week to spend with one or both parents.    _____

3    The child sees his/her extended family (aunt/uncle, cousins, grandparents, etc.) at least once a week.    _____

3    The child has a close relationship with one or more siblings.    _____

3    The family has weekly "rituals" of events that it does as a unit (e.g., a religious ritual,
     playing a game every Friday night, etc.).    _____

3    The family has specific and regularly-scheduled meetings to talk about family issues and concerns.    _____

3    The child has regularly-scheduled chores or other responsibilities.    _____

3    The child lives in an "organized household" where events are planned and scheduled, TV time is
     monitored, meals occur at a regular time, etc.    _____

## Community:

2    The child has one "best friend," with whom he/she spends some time almost every day.    _____

2    The child has a group of friends with whom he/she shares activities at least once a week.    _____

2    The child participates regularly in a religious school or service.    _____

2    The child experiences frequent success in school.    _____

2    The child has frequent successful experiences in the community (e.g. sports, clubs, etc.).    _____

*Other Coping Mechanisms* (please fully describe and enter an appropriate numerical rating):

_____

_____

_____

_____

Total Coping Score _____

## Scoring

To obtain a combined total score, you should subtract the score for Part II (Coping Mechanisms) from the score for Part I (Stress Factors). You should then note any extenuating factors.

Total Stress Score: _____ (= Stress Score_____- Coping Score)

## Interpretation

Because this scale has not yet been "normed" on a large sample, the total stress score should be interpreted cautiously. Generally, we believe that a score of 20-30 should be a cause for concern, and a score above 30 should suggest immediate intervention to help a child deal with stress.

No matter what the score, it is important to help the child find ways to reduce stress in his/her life and seek developmentally appropriate ways to handle the stresses that cannot be avoided or controlled.

# Fair Fighting Score Card

Make one card for each person practicing Fair Fighting.

Name _____

Age _____

Date _____

Name of Person Scoring_____

**Mark a plus sign below each time a person:**

_____ States what he/she wants.

_____ States what the other person(s) wants.

_____ Uses "caring language" such as an ,apology, or statement of caring.

_____ Asks non-judgmental questions to clarify a point.

_____ Accepts criticism calmly.

_____ Asks "what can I do differently?"

_____ Brings the conversation back to the problem.

_____ Listens quietly while another person talks..

**Mark a minus sign below each time a person:**

_____ Any type of physical fighting

_____ Blaming

_____ Interrupting others.

_____ Puts words in another person's mouth.

_____ Uses a threatening tone of voice.

_____ Name-calling

_____ Not listening

_____ Trying to get revenge

_____ Excuse making

_____ Not taking responsibility

Subtract the minus signs from the plus signs to get:

Total Points _____

# Fighting Fair Flash Cards

Glue or tape these cards onto 3" x 5" index cards for greater durability.

## 1. Focus on the problem.

State what is really bothering you.

## 2. Attack the problem, not the person

Use caring and respectful language

## 3. Listen with an open mind.

Do not interrupt. Do not use harsh language or a threatening tone of voice. Allow for disagreement.

# Fighting Fair Flash Cards

## 4. Treat the other person with respect.

Frequently restate the other person's point of view to show that you are listening.

## 5. Take responsibility for your reaction

Do not blame others, but focus on what you can do to solve the problem.

## 6. Do not commit "fouls"

(name-calling, blaming, any physical contact, threats, and so on)

# History of Interventions

Name of Child: _____

Name(s) of Parent(s) Being Interviewed: _____

_____

Date:_____

Name of Technique: _____

Length of Time: _____

Approximate Dates: _____

Parents' Understanding of Techniques:_____

_____

_____

How the Technique was Learned: _____

_____

Reason(s) the Technique was Unsuccessful:

      1._____

      _____

      2._____

      _____

      3._____

      _____

Therapist's Comments: _____

_____

_____

_____

# Mentoring Contract

I _____ agree to act as a mentor for

_____ who will be my student for a period

from _____ (date) to _____ (date).


During this time we will meet _____ hours per week* at the following times:

_____

_____

_____


We agree that  following are activities that will be both instructive and fun to do together.

_____

_____

_____


Signed

Mentor _____ (Date) _____

Student _____ (Date) _____


*A minimum of 3 hours

# Peer Mediation Flash Cards

Glue or tape these cards onto 3" x 5" index cards for greater durability.

**Be Willing to Solve the Problem**

**Tell the Truth**

**Listen Without Interrupting**

# Peer Mediation Flash Cards

**Be Respectful;
No Name-Calling
or Fighting**

**Take
Responsibility for
Carrying Out Your
Agreement**

# Relaxation Chart

These ar the  steps to relax your body and mind:

1. Find a quiet place and a comfortable chair.

2. Breathe deeply and slowly.

3. As you do this relax each of your muscle groups, one at a time—your shoulders, your back, your stomach, your thighs, your neck, your arms and hands, your legs and feet.

4. Now that you are relaxed your body should feel very comfortable and you can either listen to quiet soothing music or take an imaginary trip in your mind to a relaxing place like a beach or a quiet field.

5. After you have relaxed for 10 or 15 minutes, you should slowly get up and do something that is both fun and productive!

| | Monday | Tuesday | Wednesday | Thursday | Friday | Saturday | Sunday |
|---|---|---|---|---|---|---|---|
| Time spent relaxing | | | | | | | |
| Rate how relaxed you felt on a 1-10 scale | | | | | | | |

1 = very tense

10 = completely relaxed

# Self Report Problem Checklist

List the behaviors that you want to change in Column 1.

Each day rate each behavior on the following 7-point scale

1= The problem is severe
2= The problem is bad but tolerable
3= I can cope with the problem
4= The problem is definitely better
5= The problem is almost gone
6= The problem is hardly there
7= The problem is gone

| Problem Behavior | 1 | 2 | 3 | 4 | 5 | 6 | 7 | 8 | 9 | 10 | 11 | 12 | 13 | 14 | 15 | 16 | 17 | 18 | 19 | 20 |
|---|---|---|---|---|---|---|---|---|---|---|---|---|---|---|---|---|---|---|---|---|
| | | | | | | | | | | | | | | | | | | | | |
| | | | | | | | | | | | | | | | | | | | | |
| | | | | | | | | | | | | | | | | | | | | |
| | | | | | | | | | | | | | | | | | | | | |
| | | | | | | | | | | | | | | | | | | | | |

# Stop Light Card

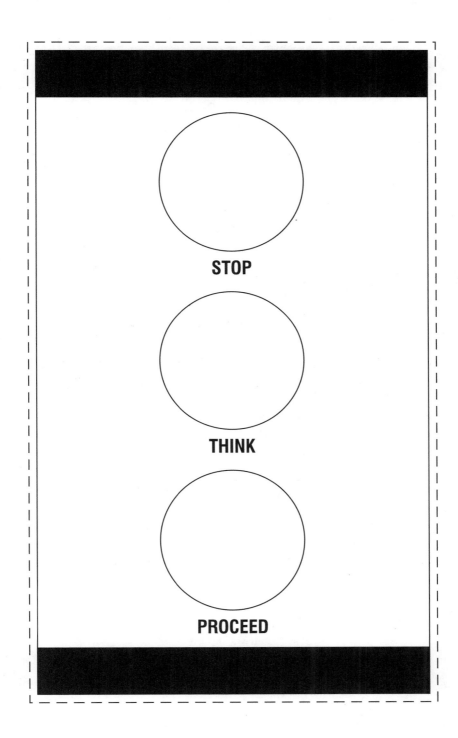

# Time-Out Worksheet

Name of Child _____

Age of Child _____ Years

Length of Time-Out_____ Minutes (1 minute for each year of child's age)

Location of Time-Out Center _____

Behavior to Regulate: (Pick 1 to 3 specific, problematic behaviors)

1. _____

2. _____

3. _____

Record the number of Time-Outs given in a week:

| Problem Behavior | Day | Time | Child's Attitude |
|---|---|---|---|
|  |  |  |  |
|  |  |  |  |
|  |  |  |  |
|  |  |  |  |
|  |  |  |  |
|  |  |  |  |
|  |  |  |  |
|  |  |  |  |
|  |  |  |  |
|  |  |  |  |
|  |  |  |  |

# Triple Column Technique Form

**Examples:**

| Automatic Thought | Cognitive Distortion | Rational Response |
|---|---|---|
| 1. I'm all alone in the world | This is th way I feel, but it is not really true. | I feel lonely, but there are many people I care about, and who care about me. But I still feel I want more. There are things I can do about this. |
| 2. I'm doing lousy in school. There is no reason to try and study harder and go to college. | I am maximizing my failures. | I'm doing poor in some subjects, but well in others. Everyone has strengths and weaknesses. |

| Automatic Thought | Cognitive Distortion | Rational Response |
|---|---|---|
| | | |
| | | |
| | | |
| | | |
| | | |
| | | |
| | | |